CAREER SKILLS LIBRARY

Problem Solving

THIRD EDITION

Communication Skills

Finding A Job

Leadership Skills

Learning the Ropes

Organization Skills

Problem Solving

Professional Ethics and Etiquette

Research and Information Management

Teamwork Skills

FERGUSON

CAREER SKILLS LIBRARY

Problem Solving

THIRD EDITION

Ferguson Publishing
An imprint of Infobase Publishing

Problem Solving, Third Edition

Copyright ©1998, 2004, 2009 by Infobase Publishing

Ferguson
An imprint of Infobase Publishing
132 West 31st Street
New York NY 10001

Problem solving. — 3rd ed.
    p. cm. — (Career skills library)
  Includes bibliographical references and index.
  ISBN-13: 978-0-8160-7773-1 (hardcover : alk. paper)
  ISBN-10: 0-8160-7773-8 (hardcover : alk. paper) 1. Vocational guidance.
2. Problem solving. 3. Career development. 4. High school graduates—
Employment. I. Ferguson Publishing.
  HD30.29.M33 2009
  650.1—dc22   2009003909

Ferguson books are available at special discounts when purchased in bulk quantities for businesses, associations, institutions, or sales promotions. Please call our Special Sales Department in New York at (212) 967-8800 or (800) 322-8755.

You can find Ferguson on the World Wide Web at http://www.fergpubco.com

Text design by David Strelecky, adapted by Erik Lindstrom
Cover design by Cathy Rincon
First edition by Joe Mackall

Printed in the United States of America

MP FOF 10 9 8 7 6 5 4 3 2 1

This book is printed on acid-free paper.

CONTENTS

INTRODUCTION

The best way to escape from a problem is to solve it.

—Alan Saporta

One thing is for certain in an ever-changing world: There will always be problems to solve. You solve problems every day of your life. Without realizing it, you've probably developed quite a few problem-solving skills.

For example, say you plan to take the bus to school, but you miss it. You know you're in trouble. And that's one problem-solving skill—the ability to identify the problem.

Immediately you consider your options. You could walk the five miles to school. You could ride your bicycle or use in-line skates. Your friend might pick you up, you could ask your mom or dad for a ride, or you could skip school. Coming up with lots of possible solutions is another problem-solving skill.

Maybe you decide the best solution is to use your mom's car. But you run into another problem. Your brother has asked for the car first. You strike a deal with him. You agree to help him practice his tennis serve on Saturday. He agrees to let you drive to school this morning. You've used another problem-solving skill—negotiation.

You dash to the car (you can still make it to school on time), jump in, and turn the key in the ignition. Nothing happens. The car won't start. You consider the possibilities and form a theory that the problem may be caused by a weak battery. Mom is famous for leaving the inside car light on. Sure enough, you check it out and find the light still turned on. You've successfully researched, formed a hypothesis, and confirmed your theory—all problem-solving skills.

Now you can fix the problem with another problem-solving skill—an action plan. You pull out the jumper cables and jump start the car. In minutes you're on your way, thanks to problem-solving skills you didn't even know you possessed.

☞ FACT

On many employee evaluation forms, the category "Problem-Solving Abilities" takes up more room than any other evaluated trait.

Employers seek people who can handle the minor irritations and the major problems that are a part of every business. What do you do when a customer comes to you with a problem? Can you help when your work team runs into production problems? Could you help save your company from losing its

TEN PROBLEMS YOU MAY HAVE HAD BEFORE YOU LEFT HOME TODAY

1. Alarm didn't go off

2. Fell back to sleep

3. Sister hogged the bathroom

4. No milk or cereal in the house

5. Nothing for lunch (and school lunch sounds horrible)

6. Brother tells you that he won't take you to school

7. Storm knocked out power (no lights, hair dryers, curling irons, etc.)

8. Favorite shirt is too wrinkled to wear

9. Shoelace breaks

10. Forgot to do your homework

competitive edge? No matter where your career leads you, you'll move faster and higher up the ladder of success if you're perceived as an effective problem solver.

This book covers the following valuable problem-solving skills:

- Building a reputation as a problem solver, using skills that you already have, as well

No matter where your career leads you, you'll move faster and higher up the ladder of success if you're perceived as an effective problem solver.

as learning to avoid negative problem-solving behaviors

- Using analytical and critical thinking (left-brain activities) to analyze and solve problems scientifically

- Solving problems creatively by brainstorming, asking questions, approaching problems from odd angles, note-taking, and visualizing—all right brain activities

- Avoiding problem-solving potholes and pitfalls such as logical fallacies, which are errors in rational thought

- Solving problems with the Problem-Solving Process, which involves the following steps:

  1. Identifying and defining problems as people, organizational, mechanical, or many-sided in nature

  2. Defining goals and objectives

  3. Generating solutions by using brainstorming techniques such as word association, clustering, and freewriting

DID YOU KNOW?

Seventy percent of employers surveyed by The Conference Board in 2006 rated high school graduates as deficient in critical thinking/ problem-solving skills.

Source: Are They Really Ready to Work?

4. Developing a plan of action

5. Following through on a problem-solving plan by planning for contingencies, troubleshooting, learning from mistakes, and maintaining flexibility as you are solving the problem

- Applying problem-solving skills to the decision-making process

PART I

Problem-Solving Tools

1

THE PROBLEM SOLVER IN YOU

In Los Angeles, California, a luxurious high-rise apartment building was on the brink of bankruptcy. Tenant after tenant turned in notice and moved out. To owners of the building, the mass exodus made no sense. Their beautiful, well-kept apartments offered a sound bargain in a safe neighborhood. So why were people abandoning what should have been a renter's paradise?

The building's management company hired a problem-solving group to get to the bottom of the mystery. After interviewing residents and former residents, the problem-solving team presented its findings: People were moving out because the apartment elevators were too slow.

A team of troubleshooters flew in to solve the problem. They gathered cost and labor estimates on several options, from repairing the old elevators to putting in new ones. But every option proved too expensive.

✔ TRUE OR FALSE?

Are You a Good Problem Solver?

1. A customer has a problem with his order. I'm not responsible, so it's not my problem.

2. Problems can only be solved by using mathematical and scientific approaches.

3. You will always be able to find a job if you're a creative problem solver.

Test yourself as you read through this chapter. The answers appear on page 22.

Defeated, the management company had just about decided to sell the building, when the youngest member of the team took a creative look at the problem. The real problem, he suggested, wasn't the elevators. The real problem was that tenants got bored waiting for the elevators. His solution? Entertain tenants who were waiting for the elevator. Install flat-screen monitors that flashed the day's top headlines, weather, sports results, and even a trivia question or two. Pipe music into the elevator waiting areas. Add tasteful yet provocative paintings and sculptures to the waiting area to stimulate interest and discussion.

His creative solution worked. The tenants, busy reading the computer monitor, soothed by relaxing music, or admiring the art, quit complaining. The exodus ceased. The building was saved. And one creative problem solver had made his mark.

As a player for the Boston Braves, Casey Stengel watched how his manager solved the countless problems that arose during each baseball game. His success as a manager later in his career was based on the problem-solving skills he learned on the field.
(Bettmann, Corbis)

No matter what job you take, not a day will pass without some kind of problem. Certain basic skills can equip you to turn those problems into opportunities. Become a problem solver where you work, and you'll make yourself an asset to your company.

Some people make things happen. Some people watch things happen, and some people say what happened.

—**Casey Stengel, Hall of Fame baseball manager**

EVERYDAY PROBLEMS

Become a problem solver where you work, and you'll make yourself an asset to your company.

Solving problems isn't something new for you. Think of how many problems you had to solve this week:

- I can't decide what to wear to school.
- I missed my bus.
- I don't have a date to the dance on Friday.
- I need a ride to my dentist's appointment.
- My club needs to raise money or plan an event.

PROBLEM-SOLVING SKILLS YOU ALREADY USE

- Identify the problem
- Analyze the problem
- Research
- Brainstorm many options
- Think creatively
- Think logically
- Form a hypothesis
- Select the best option
- Negotiate possible pitfalls
- Troubleshoot

- The car is almost out of gas, and I'm broke.
- Somebody's in my usual seat in English class.
- I didn't pack a lunch, and they're serving meat loaf.
- There are no legal parking spots available.
- I don't understand the chemistry assignment.
- My buddy and I had a misunderstanding.
- My laptop computer won't work.
- I'm locked out of the house.
- They delivered the wrong pizza.
- I have practice after school and a report due tomorrow.

Because you solve these kinds of problems regularly, chances are you don't even realize the complex processes involved. Yet each of the preceding problems requires problem-solving skills. When you figured out what to do in each case, you had to size up the problem. You considered your options. Maybe you had to negotiate. Finally, you came up with a solution and executed it. Those are all problem-solving skills you'll need on the job.

BUILD A REPUTATION AS A PROBLEM SOLVER

Tonya got her first real job with a major airline as soon as she graduated from college. She didn't realize what a good problem solver she was until her first job evaluation. Tonya's review included these comments:

- Very resourceful—thinks of creative ways to solve problems

- Handles obstacles conscientiously

- Generates alternative solutions when solving problems

Tonya says she learned to solve problems on high school committees and on backstage crews of community theater productions. "I was the one behind the scenes, holding things together. I never got a part in a play, but I put scenery together. And if the spotlight didn't work, I'd figure something out. If we needed stairs or a window for a set and didn't have them, I'd manage to improvise."

Tonya hadn't been working at the airline long before coworkers discovered her problem-solving skills. "People started coming to me with little problems. I'd fix them. But this time, they noticed. I got a reputation as a problem solver."

DON'T TRY THIS AT WORK

Jared's first job was with a food-service company in New Jersey. He took the position because he needed the money and liked the hours. The company had a few customer-service problems, but Jared never thought that his company's problems had anything to do with him personally. After six months, Jared received his first employee evaluation:

- Isn't alert to problems
- Can't handle complex problems or identify key issues
- Slow to take action
- Needs to be persistent in problem solving
- Seldom generates more than one solution to a problem

Jared admits he deserved the poor rating. He explains, "If a customer came to me with a problem, my standard answer was, 'That's not my responsibility.' Maybe I'd tell the customer to ask somebody else. If our division didn't meet production standards, it wasn't my fault. Not my problem, I thought."

Jared's evaluation woke him up to the importance of becoming a problem solver. He started paying closer attention to his company and his customers.

PROBLEM-SOLVING SKILLS ON THE JOB

In Pittsburgh, Pennsylvania, over 1,000 high-school classrooms display a chart titled: What Do Employers Expect of Me as an Employee? Ten employer expectations follow. At the top of the list is: "Recognize problems and find solutions." The last expectation is the only one in red ink: "Read, write, and calculate well."

He began to take on problems he hadn't considered his responsibility before. And Jared's next evaluation turned out much better.

EMPLOYEE APPROACHES TO PROBLEMS

J. R. Richmond, a Midwest retailer for 40 years, believes he can tell what kind of career someone will have by the way he or she approaches a problem. Richmond divides would-be problem solvers into five groups:

- *Not my problem.* These employees ignore customers and company problems as if those problems didn't touch them personally. If they do manage to get a job, they probably won't keep it long.

- *Don't ask me.* Some people can't do simple calculations, keep a checkbook or a receipt record, or do basic math. Few employers have the time or means to teach these basic skills.

- *What now?* Some well-meaning employees can't seem to mature into independent problem solvers. They don't trust their own judgment. As a result, they bother somebody every two minutes with a problem too big for them to handle. If these employees don't change their ways and take personal responsibility for decision making, they may annoy themselves out of a job.

BOOKS ABOUT PROBLEM SOLVING

Adair, John. *Decision Making & Problem Solving Strategies.* 2d ed. London, U.K.: Kogan Page, 2007.

Fogler, H. Scott, and Steven E. LeBlanc. *Strategies for Creative Problem Solving.* 2d ed. Upper Saddle River, N.J.: Prentice Hall, 2007.

Higgins, James M. *101 Creative Problem Solving Techniques: The Handbook of New Ideas for Business.* Rev. ed. Winter Park, Fla.: New Management Publishing Company, 2005.

Kahane, Adam. *Solving Tough Problems: An Open Way of Talking, Listening, and Creating New Realities.* 2d ed. San Francisco: Berrett-Koehler Publishers, 2007.

Roam, Dan. *The Back of the Napkin: Solving Problems and Selling Ideas with Pictures.* New York: Penguin, 2008.

Treffinger, Donald J., Scott G. Isaksen, and K. Brian Stead-Dorval. *Creative Problem Solving: An Introduction.* 4th ed. Waco, Tex.: Prufrock Press, 2006.

- *Straight liner.* Straight liners know how to solve straightforward problems. They can do math and calculations and may be highly skilled professionals. But if the situation requires a new solution or any creativity, they can't handle it. They may keep their job and find a comfortable place in the company. But they shouldn't expect to advance to high levels of management.

- *Creative problem solver.* Businesses will always have spots for people who can use their creativity to solve problems. Creative problem solvers make themselves irreplaceable.

We are continually faced with a series of great opportunities brilliantly disguised as insoluble problems.

—John W. Gardner, educator and government official

Mimi Silbert grew up in a small flat in one of the poorest neighborhoods of Boston. She made her way through college and into a secure job as a therapist. She says, "As far as I can remember, I was always the person that everybody called with their problems. My job was to mediate and solve them."

But after a time, solving problems on a small scale as a therapist didn't seem enough. Ms. Silbert wanted to find a way to help more people out of poverty. She didn't believe the assumptions of others, that ex-criminals couldn't be taught values and integrity, along with job skills.

She started by taking applications from people who could barely fill out the forms. Next, she trained people who trained people, who trained people who trained people, and so on. Since 1971, over 14,000 people have found success through the Delancey Street Foundation in San Francisco. Today, Delancey Street has approximately 1,000 residents located in six facilities in New Mexico, New York, North Carolina, Massachusetts, and California (Los Angeles and San Francisco). Thousands of the nation's most "unproductive" people, according to Ms. Silbert, "have graduated into tax paying citizens leading successful lives, including truck drivers, sales people, medical professionals, realtors, mechanics, contractors . . . the President of the San Francisco Housing Commission, a deputy coroner, and a deputy sheriff." These people and others can thank Mimi Silbert, who knew how to look at an old problem in a new way.

It's up to you to decide which problem solver you'll become. If you start now to develop your problem-solving skills, your ability to come up with logical

📣 EXERCISE

Think of situations where you were required to solve a problem. What kind of problem solver were you, and what kind of problem solver are you now? The following chart lists J. R. Richmond's five types of problem solvers and offers tips on how to improve your problem-solving ability.

Type of Problem Solver	How to Improve Your Problem-Solving Skills
Not my problem	Pay attention to the needs of your customers, coworkers, and managers. Consider their problems your problems and work to help them find solutions.
Don't ask me	Learn every skill that comes along. Teach yourself new tasks, techniques, and software programs by studying books, pamphlets, and websites, as well as asking for help from friends and coworkers.
What now?	Take responsibility for decision-making in your life. Build confidence by tackling smaller problems on your own; then gradually increase the complexity of problems that you tackle until you become an independent problem solver.
Straight liner	Try to expand your creative abilities by brainstorming. Learning to be flexible with new ideas and concepts will help you tackle more challenging problems.
Creative problem solver	Continue to tackle problems head on. Remember to continue to treat all of your company's problems as your own, to hone your professional skills and education, to independently tackle problems, and to think "outside-the-box."

and creative solutions could form the foundation of a successful career. When you are confident of your problem-solving skills, you can turn each problem into an opportunity.

That's where you should start—with an attitude that expects to get things done.

IN SUMMARY . . .

* Become a problem solver at work and you will become an indispensable member of your team and company.

* The five common types of problem solvers are: Not my problem (people who ignore customers and problems that don't affect

✍ EXERCISE

* List 10 problems you solved today. What problem-solving skills did you use?

* When you have a major problem, is there somebody you go to for help? What is it about that person that makes you think he or she can handle the problem?

* Describe the biggest problem facing you right now. What skills will you need to solve it?

✔ TRUE OR FALSE: ANSWERS

Are You a Good Problem Solver?

1. A customer has a problem with his order. I'm not responsible, so it's not my problem.

False. Good employees always strive to solve any problem brought to them—regardless of whether they caused it or not. The bottom line: it's important to keep your customers happy— and solving their problems is one good way to do this.

2. Problems can only be solved by using mathematical and scientific approaches.

False. Mathematical and scientific approaches are effective problem-solving tools, but they're not the only ways to tackle a problem. A creative approach that involves consideration of out-of-the ordinary or cutting-edge solutions is usually the best approach when tackling problems that do not have one single solution.

3. You will always be able to find a job if you're a creative problem solver.

True. The workplace is full of people who ignore customer problems; lack the confidence, knowledge, or personal initiative to solve problems on their own; or who can only solve basic math- or scientific-oriented challenges. Become a valued worker by learning how to become a creative problem solver who is willing to try any approach to solve problems.

them personally); Don't ask me (people who lack the ability to learn or perform basic tasks, which hinders them from solving problems); What now? (people who have skills, but instead of solving problems on their own, keep asking their bosses for help); Straight liner (intelligent people who can't solve any problems that require flexibility or creativity); Creative problem solver (the only positive type of problem solver).

- Creative problem solvers treat all problems as if they were their own, have the ability to perform and learn simple tasks, are decisive and can solve problems on their own, and have creative and flexible minds to solve problems that are not straightforward. In addition, they are a curious people with a can-do attitudes.

2

USING SCIENTIFIC THINKING TO SOLVE PROBLEMS

T he best tool you have at your disposal for solving problems is your mind. Problem solving begins with clear thinking. And thinking comes in two varieties: scientific and creative.

Thinking is any mental activity that helps formulate or solve a problem, make a decision, or fulfill a desire to understand.

—Vincent Ryan Ruggiero in *The Art of Thinking*

Scientific thinking goes by many names: logical, critical, analytical, convergent, straight-line, and predictable. It follows certain rules of logic from Point A to Point B to Point C. Scientific thinking marches you through a hypothesis to the correct conclusion.

✔ TRUE OR FALSE?

Do You Know to Use Scientific Thinking to Solve a Problem?

1. Your brain has two distinct sides that play very different roles in the problem-solving process.

2. Using a scientific problem-solving approach would be a good way to decide on which MP3 player to purchase.

3. I won't be able to develop my scientific-thinking skills until I get to college.

Test yourself as you read through this chapter. The answers appear on pages 39–40.

Creative thinking has other names, too: inspirational, divergent, insightful, exploratory, and unpredictable. Creative thinking rockets you through new and provocative channels to shed light on new answers to old problems. (See Chapter 3 for a detailed discussion of creative thinking.)

Both types of thinking are important in your everyday problem solving, and each type comes from a different part, or side, of your brain.

USING YOUR BRAIN TO SOLVE PROBLEMS

Your brain has two sides. Each side controls certain body and thinking functions. The left side of the

Problems are to the mind what exercise is to the muscles, they toughen and make us strong.

—Norman Vincent Peale, U.S. Protestant minister and author

brain is in charge of analytical thinking or logic. It takes you through well-ordered steps and makes you the genius you are in math.

The right side operates in images and impressions rather than numbers and words. Creativity and art originate in the right brain. The chart on the next page shows how the two sides of your brain divide and conquer the unfathomable task of thinking you through life.

Good problem solvers need to draw on both sides of the brain. The young executive in Chapter 1, who solved the problem of slow elevators by installing computer screens, music, and art, used his creative right brain. But if the elevator is broken, you'll need the scientific left brain to get to the bottom of the problem and fix it.

☛ FACT

- For most people the right hemisphere of the brain controls the muscles of and receives information from the left half of the body and vice versa.

- By the time a person is 50, the brain shrinks slightly, losing about an ounce in weight.

LEFT- AND RIGHT-BRAIN COMPARISONS

Left Brain	Right Brain
Seeks one answer	Explores, seeks, examines from many viewpoints
Recognizes words	Recognizes facts or objects
Processes one stimulus at a time at lightning speed	Processes whole clusters of stimuli all at once
Orderly sequences of thought	Grasps complex wholes
A focus on parts	Takes in whole picture
Logical	Dreams
Linear thinking	Makes sense by discovering workable patterns
Organizes into units	Can connect parts of the world into fresh patterns
Governed by rules, plays by rules	Follows few rules
Draws on learned, fixed codes	Can deal with new information where no learned program is available
Organized	Sees correspondences or resemblances
Can recall complex motor sequences	Thinks in complex images
Best at implementing programs after setup	Best in initial orientation of a task

- The average human brain uses up to 20 percent of energy in the body, although it only makes up 2 percent of the body's weight.

- Many people are under the misconception that humans only use 10 percent of their brains. This is untrue; scientists have discovered a function for every part of the brain.

SURF THE WEB:
RIGHT- AND LEFT-BRAIN THINKING

Funderstanding: Right Brain vs. Left Brain
http://www.funderstanding.com/right_left_
    brain.cfm

The Human Brain: The Left and Right Brains
http://www.wright.edu/academics/honors/institute/
    brain/leftright.html

Left or Right Brain
http://www.angelfire.com/wi/2brains

Mathpower.com: Learning Styles, Culture &
    Hemispheric Dominance
http://www.mathpower.com/brain.htm

Right Brain vs. Left Brain Creativity Test
http://www.wherecreativitygoestoschool.com/
    vancouver/left_right/rb_test.htm

SOLVING PROBLEMS WITH MATH

Scientific thinking is best used when a problem requires one answer. A lot of scientific problem solving can be done with solid math skills.

Maria says she owes her employment with a large Midwest manufacturer to what she learned in math classes at school. Maria's starting job was on an assembly line, but her boss wanted to make sure she had the thinking skills she'd need if a problem did arise. Her boss also wanted to determine if she had enough thinking skills to someday be a candidate for advancement in the company. She explains: "To apply for my position, I had to take a test that looked like my high school math quizzes. My boss says I'd be shocked by how many applicants fail the test."

Ryan's ability to estimate cost and draw up a budget pushed him to the top of his training group his first year with a Texas investment firm. He explains where he acquired his skills. "I guess I started when I was eight years old and got my first allowance. Before I spent a penny, I'd write down how much I'd spend on gum, how much on candy, and how much I'd save for some great thing I wanted. I did the same kind of cost estimate when I was our high school prom committee chairperson." Ryan used his analytical thinking skills as a student and reaped the benefit in his career. Once he got to the real world, he simply combined his experiences using math as a kid with training he received in school and on the job.

A lot of scientific problem solving can be done with solid math skills.

Many problems can be solved using mathematical skills. (Marty Heitner, The Image Works)

You'll do much better in the workworld if you practice your math skills now and throughout your life.

There is always an easy solution to every human problem—neat, plausible, and wrong.

—H. L. Mencken, U.S. author, editor, and critic

FOUR STEPS OF CRITICAL THINKING

Analytical or critical thinking involves four steps:

1. Identify the problem and break it down.

2. Collect information/perform research.

MATH PROBLEM-SOLVING RESOURCES

Tao, Terence. *Solving Mathematical Problems: A Personal Perspective.* New York: Oxford University Press, 2006.

Zaccaro, Edward. *Becoming a Problem Solving Genius: A Handbook of Math Strategies.* Bellevue, Iowa: Hickory Grove Press, 2006.

Zeitz, Paul. *The Art and Craft of Problem Solving.* Hoboken, N.J.: Wiley, 2006.

3. Form opinions (hypotheses).

4. Draw conclusions.

To see how this process works, try this scenario. What would you do?

One afternoon 50 students at your high school come down with stomach cramps and vomiting. All of them ate the school-lunch chicken fingers. Those who didn't eat the chicken fingers didn't get sick. What do you conclude?

If you've already decided it was the chicken fingers, think again, Sherlock. Use the four steps of critical thinking instead of jumping to the obvious conclusion.

1. *Identify the problem.* Your classmates are sick, and you want to find out what caused the problem.

EXCERPT FROM A MANUFACTURER'S APPLICATION TEST

1. Reduce these fractions to their lowest terms:

   A. 10/32   =   _____

   B. 72/128   =   _____

   C. 19/64   =   _____

2. Subtract these fractions and reduce the answers to the lowest terms:

   A. $9\ ^{14}/_{16} - 5\ ^{6}/_{16} =$ _____

   B. $7\ ^{14}/_{16} - 4\ ^{6}/_{16} =$ _____

3. Add these decimals:

   A. 1.47 + 16.235 + 7.16 + .21 = _____

   B. 10.245 + .479 + .2 + 4.1 = _____

4. Convert these decimals to fractions:

   A. .0938   =   _____

   B. .2656   =   _____

   C. 1.32   =   _____

(See the end of the chapter for answers.)

2. *Collect information/investigate.* So you found out that the chicken-finger-eaters got sick and the brown baggers didn't. Keep going.

Ask questions that will lead you scientifically to a conclusion before you leap to one. Did some students who ate the chicken fingers not end up vomiting? Did all the chicken-finger-eaters use a particular type of sauce—such as barbecue or honey? Did other food—such as fries or macaroni salad—come with the chicken fingers? Were all the sickies from the same lunch period?

Expand your research to the kitchen. Did the same cafeteria server prepare hamburgers and chicken fingers? Did only one server prepare the chicken fingers? Did anyone in the kitchen get sick? In the past, were any complaints regarding sanitary conditions in your school's kitchen filed with your state health department? Are there any toxic substances near the chicken finger preparation area? What about pans and serving platters? Are there uncooked chicken fingers or other types of raw food lying around? Never shortcut the information gathering step during a scientific investigation.

3. *Form your hypothesis.* Maybe, after all your investigation, you still blame the chicken fingers. Perhaps, you decide, the chicken fingers are contaminated by a harmful bacteria that formed as a result of improper refrigeration or insufficient cooking. In your opinion, the chicken

fingers are responsible for the illness that afternoon. That's your theory, your hypothesis.

4. *Draw your conclusions.* The fourth step is the time to test your theory and confirm your hypothesis or adjust your conclusion. If you're brave, you might run your own experiment and eat one of the suspect chicken fingers (but since you don't know

✍ EXERCISE

• Which of the following problems can best be solved through scientific thinking?

   A. You plan to buy a new mountain bike and don't know which bike to get.

   B. You've made a date to go to the drive-in on Saturday night, but you don't have a car.

   C. You have to drive to the orthodontist's right after school and you don't know the fastest way to get there.

   Answer: A and C require scientific thinking. By gathering information, you should be able to arrive at the best mountain bike for you—one best answer. And, although many roads lead to the orthodontist's office, only one route is fastest. (As far as your carless drive-in date, you're going to need as much creativity as possible to get you out of that one.)

what caused the illness and people are really sick, this might not be such a great idea!).

You decide that you're not brave, so you don't eat the chicken finger. You decide to ask your science teacher to run a substance analysis to confirm your hypothesis. You and your teacher use a microscope to check for the presence of harmful bacteria and,

- Pretend you're buying a new car. Use the four-step scientific method. Write a sentence or two describing what you'll do for each stage.

- Have you ever jumped to a conclusion when trying to solve a problem? Which of the four steps of critical thinking did you skip? How would you solve the problem differently if you could do it again?

Microsoft founder Bill Gates is just one of countless inventors who used scientific thinking to solve problems and create groundbreaking products.
(Christof Stache, AP Photo)

lo and behold, you discover the bacteria Staphylococcus aureus, which causes gastroenteritis (inflammation of the stomach and intestinal linings). Case solved!

THE SOCRATIC METHOD

The Greek philosopher Socrates developed a powerful teaching method that is still used today in

CAREERS FOR PROBLEM SOLVERS

Are you a good problem solver, but unsure of careers that require this important skill? If so, you should visit the Skills Search section of O*NET Online, a U.S. government resource for occupational information. By selecting at least one of 10 basic skills (including mathematics and science skills), complex problem solving skills, four resource management skills, six social skills, three system skills, and 11 technical skills, you can find careers that are a good match for your skills. Some in-demand careers that require complex problem solving skills include:

- Actuaries

- Airline pilots, copilots, and flight engineers

- Biomedical engineers

- Civil engineers

- Computer software engineers, systems software

- Construction carpenters

scientific problem solving. The Socratic Method, according to author Norris Archer Harrington, "is a conversation, a discussion, wherein two or more people assist one another in finding the answers to difficult questions." These series of questions are at the heart of scientific, or critical, thinking.

In his book, *Critical Thinking: How to Prepare Students for a Rapidly Changing World,* Richard Paul

- Criminal investigators and special agents
- Financial analysts
- General and operations managers
- Industrial engineers
- Medical equipment repairers
- Microbiologists
- Network systems and data communications analysts
- Police detectives
- School psychologists
- Urban and regional planners
- Veterinarians

In fact, more than 190 careers are listed, with information on job responsibilities and other necessary skills provided for each job. Visit http://online. onetcenter.org to use this useful career exploration tool.

breaks down the Socratic Method into six types of questions. These are

1. Questions of clarification

2. Questions that probe assumptions

3. Questions that probe reasons and evidence

4. Questions about viewpoints or perspectives

5. Questions that probe implications and consequences

6. Questions about the question

Consider these categories as your scientific thought process to solve problems. For Paul's list of detailed questions that fall under each category, visit http://www-ed.fnal.gov/trc/tutorial/taxonomy.html.

DEVELOPING YOUR SCIENTIFIC THINKING SKILLS

What can you do now to develop your scientific thinking? Plenty. Take math and science, for one thing. Start budgeting your personal finances. Try going through the four steps of critical thinking the next time you have a problem that needs an answer. And the next time you see the love of your life talking to somebody new, don't jump to conclusions. Use your scientific thinking skills to investigate.

✔ TRUE OR FALSE: ANSWERS

Do You Know to Use Scientific Thinking to Solve a Problem?

1. Your brain has two distinct sides that play very different roles in the problem-solving process.

True. The left side of your brain controls analytical, or logical, thought. The right side of your brain controls creative thought. Good problem solvers use both sides of their brains to solve problems.

2. Using a scientific problem-solving approach would be a good way to decide on which MP3 player to purchase.

True. Use scientific problem solving to gather fact-based information (such as each MP3 player's hard drive space, price, playback features, etc.) that will help you determine one best answer (such as which MP3 model to buy). Your creative problem-solving skills will kick in when you need to choose a color or a model design—or when you realize you don't have any money and will need to brainstorm ways to convince your parents to buy the MP3 player for you.

3. I won't be able to develop my scientific-thinking skills until I get to college.
False. It's never too early to begin honing your

scientific problem-solving skills. In high school, take science and math classes, participate in science clubs, manage your finances, and practice the four steps of critical thinking: (1) Identify the problem and break it down, (2) Collect information/perform research, (3) Form opinions (hypotheses), and (4) Draw conclusions.

IN SUMMARY . . .

- Become a problem solver at work and you will become an indispensable member of your work team and company.

- Problem solving begins with two types of thinking: scientific and creative.

- Your brain is divided into left and right sides. The left brain manages analytical thinking and logic. The right brain works in images and impressions, managing creative and artistic thinking. The left and right brains work together to help you solve problems.

- You can improve your scientific problem-solving abilities by developing solid math skills.

- Analytical or critical thinking involves four steps: (1) identifying and breaking down a problem, (2) collecting information and performing research, (3) forming an

ANSWERS TO EXCERPT FROM A MANUFACTURER'S APPLICATION TEST

1. Reduce these fractions to their lowest terms:

   A. 10/32 = 5/16

   B. 72/128 = 9/16

   C. 19/64 = 19/64

2. Subtract these fractions and reduce the answers to the lowest terms:

   A. $9\,^{14}/_{16} - 5\,^{6}/_{16} = 4\,^{1}/_{2}$

   B. $7\,^{14}/_{16} - 4\,^{6}/_{16} = 3\,^{1}/_{2}$

3. Add these decimals:

   A. 1.47 + 16.235 + 7.16 + .21 = 25.075

   B. 10.245 + .479 + .2 + 4.1 = 15.024

4. Convert these decimals to fractions:

   A. .0938 = 469/5000

   B. .2656 = 166/625

   C. 1.32 = 33/25

opinion (hypothesis), and (4) drawing conclusions.

- It's never too early to develop your scientific-thinking skills. Take plenty of mathematics and science courses in high school; start budgeting your personal finances and applying the four steps of critical thinking to any problem you have.

3

USING CREATIVE THINKING TO SOLVE PROBLEMS

Now it's time to get creative. For which of the following problems will you need to apply a hefty dose of right-brained, creative thinking?

1. Your graduating class needs to come up with a class motto.

2. You don't know where to take your date on Friday night.

3. You need a prom theme.

4. You didn't do your homework, and you need an excuse fast.

Answer? All of the above. Creative thinking explores the possibilities. It examines the problem from as many angles as possible. When you need lots of ideas—for a class motto, a date, a prom

Creative thinking explores the possibilities. It examines the problem from as many angles as possible.

✔ TRUE OR FALSE?

Do You Know to Use Creative Thinking to Solve a Problem?

1. When solving problems, never accept the situation at face value and always think outside the box.

2. Creative thinking only comes during brainstorming sessions.

3. Not everyone is creative.

Test yourself as you read through this chapter. The answers appear on page 55.

theme, or a homework excuse—you need to use creative or divergent thinking.

―――――――――――――――――

There are no problems—only opportunities to be creative.

—Dorye Roettger

THINKING OUTSIDE THE DOTS

Try this universal thinking exercise. Make nine dots on a sheet of paper. Without lifting your pencil, can you draw four straight lines to connect the dots? See the answer at the end of this chapter.

Most people can't solve the dot problem; they restrict themselves in their thought processes. They don't allow themselves to go outside the dots. Rather than taking you in a direct path of thought, creative thinking takes you off that beaten path, sometimes to a place where no person has gone.

Creative thinking comes into use when you need new solutions to old problems. Imagine this: It's the day you've dreaded. You have to get up in front of your entire second-period class and give a report on the Dinka tribe of Sudan. You're prepared, but in the hall on your way to class, you catch the hem of your pants and the hem pulls out. You have to fix it, but there's no needle, no thread. What do you do?

Using needle and thread would be easy. But you have to think outside the dots. Without reading further, see how many ideas you can come up with.

Okay. Here are some possibilities to use in repairing your hem: staple, tape, pin, paper clip, string, safety pin, bobby pin, barrette, garbage bag ties, paste, glue, jelly, gum, peanut butter, and melted Snickers; you can even trade clothes with a friend.

With a little creative thinking, the possibilities are endless.

☞ FACT

You don't have to have a high IQ to be a good thinker. Renowned psychologist E. Paul Torrance discovered that fully 70 percent of all creative people score below 135 on IQ tests.

THE "IDEA WOMAN"

Marcella is a second-year shipping clerk who believes in the power of creative thinking. "In high school, nobody thought of me as especially creative. But when our class was in charge of homecoming, the prom, or our senior trip, I always had a lot of ideas to offer." When she graduated, Marcella took a job that involved supplying large companies with stationery and other office supplies.

Marcella says her habit of coming up with a lot of ideas quickly made her an asset. "I discovered that shipping clerks had to get creative when supply didn't exactly meet demand. When we ran short of green pens, I'd think of options to the usual slow back-order notification: call the customer and apologize, give a discount on another color, offer to send what we had. Pretty soon, I was the 'Idea Woman.'"

Marcella had developed her own techniques for creative thinking. And her creativity secured her job. If your thinking is in a rut (and even if it's not), try the techniques discussed in the following sections to spark your creativity.

No great discovery is ever made without a bold guess.

—Sir Isaac Newton, English mathematician and physicist

BRAINSTORMING

Brainstorming is the process of rapidly spilling out every idea imaginable. Chapter 7 deals in greater detail with methods of brainstorming. But for now, imagine your boss has asked you to come up with a new name for your product. Scientific thinking will not produce the answer. You need to come up with as many possibilities as you can. Then you can choose the best one. You can use the process of brainstorming to help you generate ideas. You might sit in a room with your coworkers, staring at the product and yelling out ideas. You might sit at your desk with a pad of paper, writing down anything that pops in your head. Or you might think of other creative ways to brainstorm new ideas. The key is to use the creative side of your brain, not the scientific side.

ASKING QUESTIONS

It's obvious that these letters spell "THE CAT," right?

THE CAT

Asking questions can be a great way of stirring your creative thoughts.

But take a closer look. The H and A are the same. Yet you saw what you expected to see in this example adapted from O. G. Selfridge's *Pattern Recognition and Modern Computers*.

When you hit a problem, make sure you're seeing it clearly. Asking questions can be a great way of stirring your creative thoughts. Don't accept everything at face value. Challenge assumptions.

Suppose your teacher tells the class that because there has been too much talking, you must all decide your own punishment. But while the rest of the class is trying to devise weak forms of punishment, you ask questions: Was there too much talking? How about compared with other classes? What's too much anyway? Who did the talking? Why were they talking? What kind of talking? And why was talking so bad anyway? Would it have been okay if the teacher had talked with them or if people had talked about the "right" subject? What if the class had designated talking breaks, 60 seconds when you could talk to anybody about anything? That wouldn't be too much, would it? Is talking the real problem?

If the only tool you have is a hammer, you tend to see every problem as a nail.

—Abraham Maslow, U.S. author and psychologist

Of course, there's a time to keep your questions to yourself, and a wise person knows when. But you can cultivate the art of questioning all day long.

TURNING THINGS UPSIDE DOWN

When everybody else is analyzing a problem in the same way and getting nowhere, turn the whole thing upside down. Kevin works on a manufacturing team that is responsible for producing a set number of pump parts per week. When his team failed to meet its goal four weeks in a row, the team met to try to solve the problem.

Kevin explains what happened next. "We went round and round and got nowhere. First, we looked at our own performance, but we knew we couldn't go any faster. Our boss suggested we might have to get higher-power equipment to get the pieces out of the plant faster."

That's when Kevin turned the whole thing upside down. "Instead of looking at us or the machinery, I looked at our spread table [where pieces were placed for assembly]. All of a sudden it hit me. If we had an L-shaped table, we could cut out one step. Nobody had ever thought of it before."

Kevin's team made its goal with an afternoon to spare. Their boss rewarded the team's creativity by letting them go home early every Friday, as long as they'd reached their production goal.

THE EVER-PRESENT NOTEBOOK

Creative thinking doesn't always come on demand. Some of the world's best ideas have come in odd places, like bathtubs and under apple trees. It's a good idea to carry a small notebook around with you. At least keep a notepad by your bedside, in your car, and next to your shower. Too often that right brain clicks in when you're least prepared. Don't miss your best ideas simply because you didn't write them down.

VISUALIZING

No two problems are alike. Try a different point of view. Be radical.

Visualizing is a technique we'll talk more about later. Your creative mind can take in the big picture. Try picturing how things will look when your problem is solved. You want a pet, but you don't know which pet to get. Can you visualize yourself in your room, happy with your . . . what? Your iguana? Your cat, dog, snake, camel? But you better combine your creative

SURF THE WEB: DEVELOP YOUR CREATIVE THINKING SKILLS

10 Steps for Boosting Creativity
http://www.jpb.com/creative/creative.php

Creativity Foundation
http://creativity-found.org/index.html

Creativity Portal
http://www.creativity-portal.com/bc

How to Unleash Your Creativity
http://www.sciam.com/article.cfm?id=how-to-
    unleash-your-creativity

Mind Tools: Creativity Tools
http://www.mindtools.com/pages/main/newMN_
    CT.htm

thinking with scientific thinking before you make your purchase.

Visualizing, or imaging, may give you the edge to come up with that multimillion-dollar new product. Can't you picture designer water for dogs? All the shelves right above the dog food in your local supermarket stacked with rows of your creation, "Pure Puppy" or is it "Doggie Dew"?

No two problems are alike. Try a different point of view. Be radical. For years companies tried to cut employee insurance expenses. They explored cheaper healthcare providers, poorer coverage, and higher co-payments. Then one executive turned the whole thing upside down. Why not work on getting employees to be healthier? Then they won't need so much care. They built an exercise room and started company weight-loss bonus programs. Medical costs went down.

Creativity is inventing, experimenting, growing, taking risks, breaking rules, making mistakes, and having fun.

—Mary Lou Cook, educator

CREATIVITY AND YOU

Perhaps you think you're not the creative type, that you lack an "artistic" sensibility. Well, think again. True, some people are more creative than others, but we all start out with a degree of creativity. Children are curious by nature. They ask questions and come up with wild ideas. They can imagine what it might be like to fly like a bird or sit on a cloud.

Now is the time to recapture that child-like curiosity. Have some fun. Let yourself be ridiculous. Ask 20 questions a day about things you've always taken for granted. Why do clocks run clockwise? Why are there only nine numbers and a zero to work with? Why is bacon cut in strips? Why don't they make a microwave cooling appliance to freeze things instantly?

The man who asked himself as he drove home in a light drizzle, "Why don't they make windshield wipers that pause for light rain?" is a millionaire today. He took his idea (and his patent) to automobile manufacturers and cashed it in.

In order to be a top-notch coder, you must have good problem-solving skills. So much of coding is in the 'gray area,' and it takes someone who can analyze the chart note and identify the appropriate codes to report. A coder who is also performing a billing function, getting the claims paid, working denials, and identifying errors is key to medical coding.

—Deborah Grider, president of the National Advisory Board of the American Academy of Professional Coders and owner of Deborah Grider & Associates LLC, a health care consulting firm

SURF THE WEB: CREATIVITY AT WORK

10 Steps to a More Creative Office
http://www.jpb.com/creative/office_creativity.php

Creativity at Work
http://www.creativityatwork.com

✍ EXERCISE

- Come up with 20 questions about things you've never stopped to wonder about.

- Turn your bedroom upside down—not literally. Imagine as many ways as possible that you might rearrange your room.

- It's snowing. You have to get to school, and there are no shoes or boots in the house. Improvise. Make a list of things you could wear.

- You've hiked for miles along a narrow creek in the forest preserve near your house. The small footbridge you normally cross to return home has been heavily damaged in a storm and is unusable. Using creative thinking, how will you get across the creek and return home? Make a list of the safest and fastest options.

- Brainstorm new ways to do a common task at work or home. Use creative problem-solving methods such as thinking outside the box, asking questions, and visualizing to come up with ways to accomplish this task more quickly and in a more enjoyable manner.

CREATIVITY ON THE JOB

At your new job, your very newness may be an asset. You may come in with just the fresh point of view your team needs. Don't be intimidated. Of course, you need to respect people who have experience.

✔ TRUE OR FALSE: ANSWERS

Do You Know to Use Creative Thinking to Solve a Problem?

1. When solving problems, never accept the situation at face value and always think outside the box.
True. Never take the "facts" for granted—investigate and ask questions to learn the truth of a situation. Use every creative approach possible—especially when tackling challenging problems that can't be solved via conventional thinking.

2. Creative thinking only comes during brainstorming sessions.
False. Creative thoughts can come at any point in your day: during a dream, while you're heading to work, during lunch, when you're exercising or watching a movie, or in countless other instances. The key is to take advantage of these creative spurts by getting your ideas down on paper even if they don't make complete sense at the time. You'll have time later to hone them into coherent thoughts.

3. Not everyone is creative.
False. Although some of us may be more creative than others, we're all capable of thinking creatively to solve problems. The key is to open your mind to creative problem-solving approaches that the logical portion of your brain might typically ignore.

They may have already tried your idea, but maybe not. Don't waste a creative idea because you're afraid your coworkers won't like it. Open your mind to all the possibilities.

IN SUMMARY . . .

- Use creative thinking when you need to come up with many ideas to solve a problem and when you need to find new solutions for old problems.

- Many people have trouble solving problems because they are afraid to think "outside of the box." Thinking creatively will help you come up with solutions that no one may have ever considered.

- There are many good ways to spark your creativity and solve problems. Try brain-

SOLUTION TO DOT PUZZLE

In order to solve the problem, allow your lines to pass through the center and sides of dots and let the lines extend beyond the box of dots.

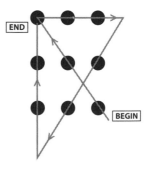

storming, asking questions, approaching a problem from an unexpected angle, carrying a notebook in case a creative thought pops up at an inopportune time, and visualizing possible solutions to a problem.

- Many people think they are not creative, but creativity is a talent that everybody has in some measure. Regain your creativity by thinking like a child and remaining open to possibilities, ideas, and scenarios that your adult mind usually closes off.

- Creativity is always an asset in the workplace. At your first job, use your youthful creativity to help solve problems. Be careful to offer your creative opinions wisely; be sure to respect the knowledge and experience of other workers.

4

OBSTACLES TO PROBLEM SOLVING

Buy our toothpaste and improve your love life.

Before I called Psychic Hotline, I was bankrupt. Now that I have my personal psychic, I've just made my first million. Call for yourself and get rid of financial worries.

If you don't contribute today, our station may go off the air. And thousands of little children will never know true joy.

Want your child to stay warm in the cold, outside world? Make him warm on the inside. Give him oatmeal.

Double your pleasure. Double your fun. Chew our gum.

What's wrong with these promises? They have helped sell millions of dollars in products and services. Some of them sound pretty good. Who

Do You Know How to Get Past Problem-Solving Obstacles?

1. The new guy at school wears glasses and a pocket protector. He must be really smart.

2. All my friends say Mr. Ramirez is a bad teacher, so I should avoid signing up for his classes.

3. Taking the highway is always faster than taking side streets.

Test yourself as you read through this chapter. The answers appear on page 71.

wouldn't want to make a million bucks and have sex appeal?

But you know better. You sense something's not quite on the up-and-up. But what's wrong? Can you pick out the exact place where these promises go wrong? Each one contains at least one error in logic. We call those wrong turns in thinking "logical fallacies."

LOGICAL FALLACIES

On the surface, it makes sense that if Jolene called a psychic and got inside information that turned her into a millionaire, you could do the same. But

WHAT IS LOGIC?

The *Encarta World English Dictionary* defines logic as "the branch of philosophy that . . . aims to distinguish good from bad reasoning."

the logic is false. Her financial success may have had nothing to do with the tip from her psychic. And even if it did, who says the same thing can happen to you?

All the facts aren't in on toothpaste and gum either. There may be more to those stories of sex appeal and pleasure. And what exactly does oatmeal have to do with keeping a kid warm as he trudges through the snow to get the school bus? Again, even if the TV station does fold because you fail to contribute, couldn't those kids find joy somewhere else?

We get ourselves (and our employers) into trouble when we take a wrong turn in thinking and follow a logical fallacy. If you're aware of the pitfalls and logical potholes out there, you'll have a better chance of avoiding them.

The following sections provide examples of some of the most common logical fallacies. They will also give you advice on how to avoid falling into common reasoning pitfalls as you solve problems.

Obstacles to Problem Solving

"Not So Fast"

Which of these two lines is longer?

If you're like most people, you assumed A was longer than B. The truth is that A and B are the same length. Line A looks longer at first glance. You need to investigate and remain open-minded to avoid the logical pitfall.

Marlene admits she fell for the "not-so-fast" fallacy more than once in high school. "I always ended up with the wrong boyfriend, for one thing," she says. "If a guy looked good and talked smooth, I figured he was for me. I wish somebody had told me, 'Not so fast.'"

But by the time Marlene joined her first work team in a real estate office, she had learned her lesson. "Even though I thought I had everybody figured out after the first day, I held back. I'd finally learned I couldn't tell a book by its cover." Marlene learned to check potential buyers out and research her facts. "Sometimes a buyer will tell me money is no problem. He dresses in trendy clothes, drives a nice car, and sounds sincere. But when I check my facts, I find out he's not what he claimed."

We get ourselves (and our employers) into trouble when we take a wrong turn in thinking and follow a logical fallacy.

> *Before you recommend or do business with another person, business, or agency, tell yourself, "Not so fast."*

Check your facts, too. Before you recommend or do business with another person, business, or agency, tell yourself, "Not so fast." Then use your logical thinking skills to find out what you need to know.

Tyrone hated the way his college acquaintances stereotyped him. He explains: "I attended an out-of-state university because they had a good journalism school and I had relatives close by. But because I'm African American and tall, the first question I'd get asked when they found out I was from out of state was, 'Are you here on a basketball scholarship?' Like there wasn't any other reason I'd be there."

The students who stereotyped Tyrone were guilty of a "not-so-fast" logical fallacy. And that can be the basis of misunderstanding and prejudice. Don't assume things about your coworkers on the basis of racial, gender, ethnic, or cultural backgrounds.

BOOKS ON LOGIC AND LOGICAL FALLACIES

Gula, Robert J. *Nonsense: A Handbook of Logical Fallacies.* Mount Jackson, Va.: Axios Press, 2002.

Priest, Graham. *Logic: A Very Short Introduction.* New York: Oxford University Press USA, 2001.

Whyte, Jamie. *Crimes Against Logic: Exposing the Bogus Arguments of Politicians, Priests, Journalists, and Other Serial Offenders.* New York: McGraw-Hill, 2004.

✍ EXERCISE

Think of a time when you were guilty of a "not-so-fast" logical fallacy. It might have involved a friend, a teacher, the new kid at school, or a group or organization. How did you stereotype this person or group initially? What made you realize you were wrong? If you could repeat the situation, how would you avoid falling into a logical fallacy?

Don't assume you know what someone likes or dislikes because you think all women do or a certain nationality doesn't.

Rush to Judgment

You've cruised through your first-quarter geometry class with a B. In the second quarter, your teacher takes a leave of absence and a substitute takes over the class. Six weeks later your parents get a warning slip with your name on it. You're failing geometry. "It's Ms. Miller's fault!" you plead. "I was doing fine until she took over. They should get rid of her. Give her the warning slip!"

This might seem to make sense. But don't rush to judgment. There could be many explanations for your lower grade. This quarter's material could be harder. Or you may have been goofing off because your teacher is just a sub. Or maybe your first teacher never graded anything and gave you all Bs. You'll never know by rushing to the easiest answer. You need to check the facts logically.

People in the business world get fired all the time because companies panic and rush to judgment. The new CEO comes in and profits drop. Out goes the new CEO, even if there are better explanations for the profit loss.

The same thing happens in the world of sports. Coaches and managers better win, or they're out of a job. Never mind that the owner of the team has lost the best players by refusing to raise salaries.

Be careful of the connections you make in your business dealings. Investigate before you rush to judgment.

The first problem for all of us, men and women, is not to learn, but to unlearn.

—Gloria Steinem, U.S. author and feminist leader

Learn to Avoid Hasty Generalizations

Kathy is failing history. Alfred is failing history. Even Zack, Brad, and Angela are failing history. Therefore, nobody can pass that history class.

That's a hasty generalization. First, maybe somebody is passing and you just don't know about it. Second, so what if nobody's passing. You could be the first!

Kyle says he comes by his stubborn nature honestly, having inherited it from stubborn parents who taught him not to give up. He remembers a time in high school when he refused to accept a hasty generalization. "My graduating class was small. We wanted to go on a senior trip together for a week. All my friends said the school would never let us. The class ahead of us didn't take one. As far back as we knew, no class had been allowed an overnight senior trip."

But Kyle refused to accept the generalization that nobody could do it. "Three of us presented our case to the board of education. They said yes. We spent a glorious week in the Ozarks."

Kyle took his determination with him to San Francisco, where he joined a public-relations team. His first account was with a soft-drink company who wanted to get a foothold in the area. "Just because Coke couldn't do it and Pepsi couldn't do it, that didn't mean we couldn't. I'd at least try and find out for myself."

Hasty generalizations are logical fallacies that assume a connection between possibly unrelated events. These often come about because people do not have the time or intellectual curiosity to go beyond the seemingly obvious and dig deeper to the root of a problem. Avoid hasty generalizations at all costs. They will limit your creativity and flexibility when it comes to solving problems.

When solving problems, dig at the roots instead of just hacking at the leaves.

—Anthony J. D'Angelo, publisher

Poisoning the Well

Poisoning the well is the logical fallacy that will keep you from making your own untainted decisions about individuals, ideas, or even companies. Instead of making up your own mind, you listen to the negative comments of someone else and allow those comments to color your logic.

I mistrust the judgment of every man in a case in which his own wishes are concerned.

—Arthur Wellesley Wellington, British statesman and general

Eric fell into this logical pothole as a sophomore in high school, but it taught him a lesson he took with him to his first job. He chose the wrong Spanish teacher. "All my friends told me to stay away from Mr. H. He gave quizzes. He doled out homework. So when I was assigned to his room, I never gave him a chance. I dropped his class and took somebody else the next semester. But I still regret it. I didn't learn anything in the other class. And the kids in Mr. H's class did."

During Eric's first month at his new job, he sensed a power struggle between his team leader and their supervisor. "Before I even met the supervisor, my team leader warned me about her: she's bossy, tough to work with. But this time I decided I'd give the supervisor a chance and decide for myself. Turned out she was tough, but she was fair."

Avoid poisoning the well by ignoring other peoples' harsh opinions about individuals, groups, or issues until you have a chance to investigate these matters yourself. You wouldn't want to be prematurely judged by someone you haven't met, so be sure to extend this courtesy to others.

Most people spend more time and energy going around problems than in trying to solve them.

—Henry Ford, U.S. automotive industry pioneer

Car Washing in the Rain
One logical fallacy is all around you. "Every time I wash my car, it rains. I'm not washing it Saturday. I don't want the big game rained out." Other logical fallacies of this type include:

- "Whenever Macy goes to the movies with us, we all end up fighting. Let's not invite her."

- "This is my lucky shirt. If I don't wear it for the match, I'll lose."

- "She reads all the time, and now she needs glasses. No way I'm going to read."

The fancy name for this logical fallacy is *ex post facto reasoning*. Because B happened after A, A must have caused B. Again, be careful about your connections. A cause and effect are more complicated than one event following another. Presidents are quick to make a connection between their presidency and a growing economy: "Since I became president, the gross national product is up!" But if the economy weakens, they claim there's no connection.

Be careful of falling into ex post facto reasoning in the workplace. Just because your office has had problems since Harry joined the team, it might not be poor Harry's fault. There might be other factors that have affected the office atmosphere. Give people the benefit of the doubt and don't jump to easy conclusions when something goes wrong. Keep an open mind and dig deeper to find the true cause of a problem.

Emotional Arguments

"Please, please! You just gotta pass me in the course. If you don't, I won't graduate. If I don't graduate, I can't go to college and my mom will die. And I'll end up with no job, no home, no future."

That's the emotional, or "you just gotta," logical fallacy. If an ex-love wants to come back to you because he or she "can't live without you," check your logic. Sort out fact from emotion. You were still cheated on and lied to, right?

Emotional arguments will come at you from all directions throughout your career. Don't lose your compassion, but don't fall into an emotional pitfall of logic either. Your coworker may urge you to lie for him because the boss will fire him if the truth comes out. Another coworker may plead with you to back her up on her proposal in a team meeting. After all, look at all she's done for you and what good friends

SURF THE WEB: LOGICAL FALLACIES

The Autonomist: Logical Fallacies, Formal and
    Informal
http://theautonomist.com/aaphp/permanent/
    fallacies.php

Fallacy Files
http://www.fallacyfiles.org

LogicalFallacies.info
http://www.logicalfallacies.info

The Nizkor Project
http://www.nizkor.org/features/fallacies

you are. Sort out the emotions. Handle the matter
and people involved with tact and compassion. But
think and act logically.

THINKING AIDS

To help you avoid the pitfalls and potholes of logical
fallacies, here's a checklist of thinking aids:

- Don't go for the easy answer. Do your
  homework. Just because Disney theme
  parks are a hit in California and Florida
  doesn't guarantee success for Disney-
  land Paris.

There's a mighty big difference between good, sound reasons and reasons that sound good.

—William E. Vaughan, American columnist and author

- Make good connections. Don't assume a cause-and-effect relationship. Investigate to discover the real explanations for successes and failures.

- Know the difference between fact and opinion. Even if an authority or expert gives you an opinion, check the facts.

- Learn to delay gratification. Don't go for the quick fix or explanation.

✐ EXERCISE

- Between your favorite TV shows, try watching television commercials and picking out the faults in their claims.

- Think about your last argument with someone. List your main points and their main points. Then sort out fact and opinion.

- When you get the urge to buy something, see if you can track your own logic. What influenced your decision and desire?

✔ TRUE OR FALSE: ANSWERS

Do You Know How to Get Past Problem-Solving Obstacles?

1. The new guy at school wears glasses and a pocket protector. He must be really smart.

2. All my friends say Mr. Ramirez is a bad teacher, so I should avoid signing up for his classes.

3. Taking the highway is always faster than taking side streets.

All false. These are examples of logical fallacies, which are wrong turns in thinking. For example, the kid with the pocket protector may just be near-sighted and being careful after a pen exploded in his shirt pocket last week. Mr. Ramirez may be an excellent teacher, but he's a hard, but fair, grader and gives quizzes frequently—two things your friends don't like. And, taking the highway is often faster than surface streets when heading to a destination, but not always. Can you think of all of the times that an accident, construction, or bad weather slowed you to a crawl on the highway? Avoid logical fallacies by steering clear of popular (often negative) opinions that are unconfirmed by fact, avoiding generalizations, jumping to conclusions, and making judgments based on emotion.

- Challenge assumptions. Are things really this way, or could you be overlooking something?

- Avoid the blame game. Fault and failure are rarely the result of one person's mistake. Explore deeper causes and ask "Why?" instead of "Who?"

- Know yourself. Don't govern your decisions based upon emotion. Learn from your mistakes. Try not to make the same mistake twice. Start now to build your resistance to logical fallacies.

IN SUMMARY . . .

- Logical fallacies are wrong turns in thinking and reasoning. They contain at least one error in logic.

- Common logical fallacies include (1) "Not so fast," (2) rush to judgment, (3) hasty generalizations, (4) poisoning the well, (5) "car washing in the rain," and (6) emotional arguments.

- To avoid logical fallacies, don't accept the easy answer or assume a cause-and-effect relationship. Pursue answers beyond the most obvious ones, and try not to confuse emotion with fact.

PART II

The Problem-Solving Process

5

STEP 1–IDENTIFY
AND DEFINE
THE PROBLEM

Before tackling a problem, always remember to identify and define it first.

An age-old business saying goes like this: "Understand the problem well enough, and the solution will present itself." In other words, before tackling a problem, always remember to identify and define it first.

Take, for example, the elevator problem in Chapter 1. Tenants are moving out of a high-rise building that has slow elevators. As soon as one thinker identifies and defines the real problem, he has his solution. The problem isn't slow elevators, but tenant boredom. The solution involves computer screens, elevator music, and art.

Although most problems are complex, it may help to divide potential problems into three groups for easier identification: people problems, organizational problems, and mechanical problems.

Are You Good at Identifying and Defining a Problem?

1. There are three types of problems: people problems, organizational problems, and mechanical problems.

2. People problems at work can destroy morale and reduce productivity.

3. Organizational problems can always be fixed.

Test yourself as you read through this chapter. The answers appear on pages 91–93.

Correctly identifying whether your problem is rooted in people, the organization, or mechanics should help you determine the right solution.

Discovery consists of seeing what everybody has seen and thinking what nobody has thought.

—Albert von Szent-Gyorgyi, Hungarian biochemist and Nobel Prize winner

PEOPLE PROBLEMS

There are three types of *people problems:* those involving you, one other person, or a group of people.

You

Imagine the kinds of problems you might run into as you start your career. That first year on the job, you may discover that *you* are your biggest problem. You may be unprepared for the required job skills, the stress of your new job, or your new life in general.

Like Alan, who took an entry-level job with an airplane manufacturer in St. Louis, you may wish you'd taken more technical classes. After three weeks on the job, Alan felt himself drowning in a sea of procedures and technical equipment and asked his boss for assistance. His boss agreed that Alan was in over his head and signed him up for evening classes. Both Alan and his boss identified the problem (not enough training) to work toward a solution.

Sarah felt her training had prepared her well for her job in telemarketing. What she wasn't prepared for were the pressures that accompanied her job. Her own unhappiness became her worst enemy. Unsure of the origin of her problems at work, she quit after three months.

Few new jobs match our high expectations. The routine of nine-to-five work may come as a letdown if you have envisioned a skyrocketing career. The company's values might challenge your personal ethics. Disappointment in your job can prove a major obstacle to career success. However, if you can narrow the vague sensation that your job isn't working out for you and identify the actual problem, you'll have a better chance at solving it.

On the other hand, unhappiness may originate at home but carry over to work. You may feel lost without your old friends. This could be your first time living on your own. Personal, financial, and relationship problems can follow you to work. If you know you are the problem, you know where to look for the solution. In this case, it's not the company that needs to change; it's you.

Working in a rapidly changing technical environment, employees at all levels find themselves dealing with complex problems. They must be capable of recognizing these problems and identifying immediate actions to solve them. Whether [solving] process problems or people problems, innovative thought and action are key to success in our business.

—Deb Browne, director, corporate training and development, APP Pharmaceuticals

Person Conflict

Another kind of people problem is a conflict between you and another person. You may run into a problem with a coworker, whether it is a personality clash, career jealousy, or unhealthy competition. Or your boss might take some getting used to. Recognizing the problem for what it is can help you handle your conflict.

Personal, financial, and relationship problems can follow you to work.

(continues on page 80)

HOW TO BE HAPPY

You can no longer completely blame your genes if you're unhappy, according to a study by Sonja Lyubomirsky, a professor of psychology at the University of California. Based on her research on identical and fraternal twins, Professor Lyubomirsky believes that 40 percent of our happiness is in our control. Another 50 percent is determined by genetics, and the remaining 10 percent is dictated by personal circumstances such as bad news (a death in the family) or good news (holding the winning ticket for a multimillion dollar lottery).

Professor Lyubomirsky has written *The How of Happiness: A Scientific Approach to Getting the Life You Want* to help people become happier and improve their lives. The advice in the book is largely based on studies of habits of people who reported being happy. Some of Lyubomirsky's suggestions include:

- Keep a "best possible self" journal. Create a list of personal goals that detail how you would like to improve yourself over the next six weeks or more.

- Learn how to cope with tough times and challenges. Life can be challenging, and how you cope with negative events will play a major role in whether or not you're happy. Learn to identify and address overly negative thoughts—perhaps writing them down and analyzing them in a journal.

- Don't think too much. Don't let dark or troubling thoughts serve as roadblocks to meeting goals and achieving emotional balance. Stay focused on positive aspects of your life, and save negative thoughts for the end of the day, when, in retrospect, they often may not seem as important.

• Enjoy the little things. Savor the walk to work, a good meal, a funny conversation. Remember these moments when you feel down.

• Be optimistic. Always believe that things can get better, while also taking concrete steps to improve any negative areas of your life.

• Don't procrastinate. Solve problems as they arrive. A pile of unsolved problems often can translate into stress and unhappiness.

Depression is a clinical medical condition and not the same as being unhappy. It is often characterized by feelings of anxiety, a loss of interest in favorite activities, difficulty in sleeping (including oversleeping), and trouble concentrating. If you think you're depressed, talk to your family physician. In addition to setting up an appointment with your doctor, you can visit the following websites to learn more about depression:

MayoClinic.com (http://www.mayoclinic.com/health/depression/DS00175), The Nemours Foundation (http://kidshealth.org/teen/your_mind/mental_health/depression.html), and the National Institute of Mental Health (http://www.nimh.nih.gov/health/topics/depression/index.shtml).

Sources: Newsweek, MayoClinic.com

(continued from page 77)

Ginny discovered personality conflicts at work could prove more dangerous than conflicts in high school. "In high school, if I didn't hit it off with someone, I didn't hang out with her. If some teacher forced us to work together on a project, I knew it would all be over when the semester ended. But a personality conflict at work can wreck everything. The other person doesn't just go away." Ginny had to learn how to work through the conflict to solve the problem.

Don't criticize others. They are just what we would be under similar circumstances.

—Abraham Lincoln, U.S. President

If you can't handle a customer, a client, or a supplier, you have a people conflict. Problems with discrimination and office romances fall into this category. When two people feud, the whole team—even the company itself—may be at risk. And if that happens, your job is at risk, too. The sooner you pinpoint the problem, the better.

Group Problems

You may run into group problems at work. Your team's morale sinks. Or your team gives into petty jealousy and fails to come together as a group. You may like each other, but fail to produce as a team and meet your goals and objectives.

SURF THE WEB: POSITIVE THINKING

Can you find happiness online? No, but the following sites may provide tips and resources to help you make yourself happy.

How to be Happy: Step-by-Step Guide to Being Happy
http://stress.about.com/od/lowstresslifestyle/ss/happy.htm

MayoClinic.com: Positive Thinking
http://www.mayoclinic.com/health/positive-thinking/SR00009

Mental Health, Self Help & Psychology Information and Resources
http://www.mental-health-matters.com

Mind Tools: Thought Awareness, Rational Thinking, and Positive Thinking
http://www.mindtools.com/redpstv.html

Positive Path Network
http://www.positivepath.net

SelfhelpMagazine
http://www.selfhelpmagazine.com/index.php

WebMD: Five Things Happy People Do
http://www.webmd.com/balance/features/five-things-happy-people-do

Worker disagreements should never reach this point. This type of behavior is completely unprofessional. Work to avoid personality conflicts in the office by discussing the problem with the other party (or parties) before it gets out of hand. (Bill Varie, Corbis)

Factions can divide a work team as one group squares off against another. Departments carry on unhealthy competition within the company. Management and labor sometimes battle over every issue. Group problems can be especially troublesome in today's workplace, where teams are an essential part of most projects.

EXAMPLES OF PEOPLE PROBLEMS

- Your lack of training

- Your own unhappiness

- Disillusionment with the job

- Personality conflict

- Unhealthy competition

- Customer conflict

- Ineffective team leader

- Factions within team, department, or corporation

- Discrimination

ORGANIZATIONAL PROBLEMS

If your boss tells you to do one thing, but your supervisor expects something else, you're caught in the middle of an *organizational problem*.

Tracy joined the art department of a mid-sized graphic-arts company. She was hired to speed production so that her department would meet deadlines. But Tracy soon discovered the department's problems ran deeper than she'd anticipated.

"I was told to increase production and speed it up. But the graphic designers already worked over-

time—as fast as I've ever seen designers work. I needed to hire more workers to get the job done, but I
couldn't get the firm to listen. The week I got there,
two designers quit, and I wasn't given authority to
replace them." In Tracy's case, people weren't the
problem; the organization was.

Other organizational problems arise when the
chain of command is unclear. When employees get
caught in the middle of power struggles, everybody
suffers. If this type of problem isn't correctly identified, people get blamed.

☛ FACT

One way to alleviate organizational problems
is to establish a chain of command. A *flowchart*
(which shows steps in a sequence of operations)

EXAMPLES OF ORGANIZATIONAL PROBLEMS

- Inability to get the resources you need to do the task
- Unclear chain of command
- Changes in the economy
- Changes in the marketplace
- Overlapping responsibilities

can be used to illustrate a corporation's hierarchy of authority.

Unpredictable changes in the marketplace or the economy can cause downsizing. You may not have the necessary power to fix organizational problems, but recognizing them can help you find your way through the maze.

MECHANICAL PROBLEMS

The third kind of problem is the *mechanical* or *technical problem*. If your hard drive crashes or your Internet connection won't work, you look for a technical solution. The more you know about computers, the better. If you know you'll need to use projectors, copiers, fax machines, scanners, or other office equipment, do all you can to become an expert.

Other mechanical problems stem from telephones, computer hardware and software, inadequate phone service, telecommunication breakdowns, fax machines, and problems on the Internet.

MANY-SIDED PROBLEMS

Many problems combine difficulties involving people, organizations, and equipment. These challenges, called *many-sided problems,* must be analyzed from every angle.

Arnette was head of the yearbook staff her senior year in high school. Her problem was that, because yearbook sales had been so low the past three years,

SURF THE WEB: HELP WITH OFFICE EQUIPMENT

Expert Village: Learn Basic Computer Skills
http://www.expertvillage.com/video-series/528_
computer-filing-system-windows.htm

How Stuff Works: How Fax Machines Work
http://communication.howstuffworks.com/fax-
machine4.htm

How Stuff Works: How Virtual Offices Work
http://communication.howstuffworks.com/virtual-
office.htm

How to Use a Scanner
http://www.aarp.org/learntech/computers/
howto/Articles/a2002-07-16-scan.html

her principal threatened to cut yearbook funds drastically.

Why were sales so bad? She needed to examine the problem from all possible angles. She and her committee considered the quality, price, timing, and advertising of the yearbooks. They analyzed the audience and discovered that almost all seniors bought a copy, but nobody else did. The staff put together a survey to find out why this was the case. They discovered that underclassmen didn't buy the yearbook because they didn't expect to see many photos of their class. Now Arnette's committee had the focus they needed. They took hundreds of photos of each class and made sure students knew their class would be represented in the new yearbook. As a result, yearbook sales nearly doubled.

After graduating from college, Arnette took a job in hotel management in Hawaii. When the hotel ran into a similar problem, Arnette remembered her yearbook success.

"The hotel was losing money. But our ads in vacation magazines had paid off. Our target audience, mainland vacationers, responded to the ads and booked holidays. We analyzed the situation and came up with the problem: a lack of specialty bookings. We expanded the audience to golfers and honeymooners—just as I'd expanded to underclassmen in high school."

THE SIX Ws

One method of analysis to identify the real problem is asking six "W" questions: who, what, when, where, why, and what if?

For example, imagine that your company has been producing the most adorable stuffed bear at the cheapest price on the market, but nobody's buying it.

- *Who* should be buying the product? Analyze your audience, run a demographic study, and put together a survey.

- *What* is your product made of? Is it made of quality materials? When you check out this angle, you discover that your bears, adorable as they may be, fall apart easily. Hence, you have a quality problem.

- *When* are you advertising and selling? Is it at the best times?

- *Where* are you selling your product? Are you reaching the right locales and putting the product on the right shelves in the right stores?

- *Why* do you charge what you charge? Why produce the number of bears that you do?

- *What if* you stopped producing bears, switched to bunnies, and made them larger or smaller or in different colors? Would that solve the problem?

If after going through these questions you still haven't found your answer, you're back to quality. Now all you have to do is figure a way to increase the quality of your product without increasing its cost. You might cut costs somewhere else, such as delivery costs, advertising, etc. But at least you have

---

He who asks a question may be a fool for five minutes, but he who never asks a question remains a fool forever.

—**Tom Connelly**

the problem clearly defined and can move ahead with the solution.

THE SWOT TEST

Another way to focus on the real problem is to run the SWOT test: Analyze the situation for **s**trengths, **w**eaknesses, **o**pportunities, and seasonal **t**hreats.

Take the failing stuffed bears. What are its strengths? They're adorable and cheap. What are the weaknesses? The bears fall apart. What opportunities are you missing for sales? Have you considered

TWO METHODS OF ANALYZING THE PROBLEM

The Six Ws	The SWOT Test
Who? (audience)	Strengths (appearance, cost)
What? (quality)	Weaknesses (quality)
When? (timing)	Opportunities (advertising)
Where? (locale)	Threats (seasonal, competition)
Why? (mission)	
What if? (options)	

advertisements, testimonials, shelf space, or offering a variety of colors? Are there any seasonal threats? Do they sell well or poorly around the holidays? Do sales drop dramatically in summer?

BE INFORMED

The only way to find answers to specific questions is to delve deeply and research the problem. Several years ago, the Red Cross began to run low on blood supplies. The obvious solution was to send out more pleas for donors. But a problem-solving team took the time to analyze the problem.

The only way to find answers to specific questions is to delve deeply and research the problem.

Why was there a shortage on blood? It wasn't an increased need for blood. The number of volunteer donors had plummeted. After surveying would-be donors to clearly define the problem, researchers discovered the real cause of the donor shortage: a fear of contracting AIDS. People knew just enough about AIDS to fear blood and needles. No amount of pleading was going to change their minds. The Red Cross decided to run a campaign to inform donors about the causes of AIDS and let the public know that because blood banks use only clean needles, there is little to no chance of contracting the disease through donating.

You know the pains and rewards of research if you've ever written a research paper. If you skimmed over secondary sources and ignored the best information available, you probably omitted key arguments and data. Your grade probably reflected your laziness.

But students are not the only ones who can stop too soon when gathering information and end up with false conclusions. In October 1967, the Soviet Union launched a space probe designed to crash on the surface of Venus and send back information about the temperature and conditions on the planet. When the space probe stopped transmitting, it was presumed the craft had hit its target. The data sent at that point indicated temperature and atmospheric pressure that could possibly sustain life as we know it!

But there was a problem that wasn't discovered until much later. The Russian craft had malfunctioned and stopped transmitting signals when it was still 15 miles from the surface of Venus. The actual Venus temperatures turned out to be 75 to 100 times that of Earth, too hot for life as we know it. Lesson: Stick with a problem until you're sure you've correctly identified and defined it.

Stick with a problem until you're sure you've correctly identified and defined it.

✔ TRUE OR FALSE: ANSWERS

Are You Good at Identifying and Defining a Problem?

1. There are three types of problems:
people problems, organizational problems, and mechanical problems.

True. People problems involve problems with yourself (lack of adequate training, workplace stress, etc.), another person (jealousy, clash in work styles, etc.), or a group of people (competing departments, cliques, etc.). Organizational problems involve unfair expectations from management, problems with chain of command, and other related issues. Mechanical problems involve problems with the technology (such as printers, fax machines, computer software and hardware) that you use to do your job.

2. People problems at work can destroy morale and reduce productivity.

True. These types of issues often fester and grow until they explode at the height of a project, production schedule, or other critical time at work. It's important to avoid problems with coworkers by keeping the lines of communication open and accepting your coworkers' personalities and work styles.

3. Organizational problems can always be fixed.

False. Some organizational problems are so large or ingrained that they can only be fixed by a major managerial housecleaning or restructuring. Others are caused by economic or marketplace trends that are too large for any company to control on its own. Even if you cannot fix these problems, it's important to be aware of them so that you can better understand your employer

and anticipate and address potential problems
before they arise.

IN SUMMARY . . .

- Most problems can be organized into one
  of three categories: people, organizational,
  or mechanical. Some challenges are a
  combination of all three types, which is
  called a many-sided problem.

- People problems can be further reduced to
  one of three types: those that involve only
  you, those that involve one other person,
  and those that involve a group.

- If you have identified an organizational
  problem, share it with a supervisor or
  someone at a higher level within the
  organization.

- While in school, try to learn as much as
  you can about equipment and technology
  (through class or work experience) to avoid
  later mechanical problems.

- Multisided problems must be analyzed
  from different angles, using questions
  such as "the six Ws" (who, what, when,
  where, why, and what if?) or the SWOT
  method (consider **s**trengths, **w**eaknesses,
  opportunities, and **t**hreats).

✍ EXERCISE

- Clearly define three real problems facing you right now. Next to each, indicate whether it's a people, mechanical, or organizational problem—or a combination of the three.

- What can you do with your remaining time in school to head off potential mechanical problems in your career?

- What kinds of people problems (including those involving only yourself) do you run into most often?

- Whatever your problem, make sure you don't settle for a half-baked solution—keep questioning until you're fully satisfied.

6

STEP 2—DEFINE GOALS AND OBJECTIVES

Before you begin to establish goals and objectives and go forward with the solution to your problem, double-check to be sure you've properly identified the problem. Sort out the cause from the effect. If you don't, your solution is bound to be incomplete.

For example, say your English grade has fallen this semester. True, that's a problem—but it's an effect. As you set your goal for the rest of the semester and determine to raise your grade, you need to explore the cause. You've always gotten As in English, so you're not incapable of scoring high marks. You've done your homework and done okay on tests. What's left? Class participation. You've been practically asleep in class lately. Could that be it?

Now you're closer to the cause. Your goals are not only going to include raising your grade; you're also going to plan to stay awake in class. But keep digging—sleeping in class is an effect of another problem. You never fell asleep in class until this semester. What's changed in your life to cause you to sleep in English class?

Then you get it. Your class starts at 8:00 A.M. and you've been staying up late every night watching television. Your goals and objectives will have to start there, maybe limiting late-night television to Friday nights.

CONNECTING GOALS TO THE REAL PROBLEM

A problem's definition should include its cause and effect.

A problem's definition should include its cause and effect. Problem: "My late-night television viewing is causing me to sleep in class and get a lower grade in English." Now you're ready to set goals that will speak to the root of the problem.

In the business world, it's important to define the problem in terms of the company's goals, in light of their overall purpose. Ask, "What caused the effect?" instead of "Whose fault is it?"

SETTING GOALS

You set goals all the time. Remember your New Year's resolutions? (Probably not if it's no longer January.) Perhaps you vowed, "This year I will lose weight, save money, and be nicer to my parents." Goals are the way you want things to look—the end product.

HELPFUL BOOKS ON ESTABLISHING AND MEETING GOALS

Bachel, Beverly K. *What Do You Really Want? How to Set a Goal and Go for It! A Guide for Teens.* Minneapolis, Minn.: Free Spirit Publishing, 2001.

Dobson, Michael S., and Susan B. Wilson. *Goal Setting: How to Create an Action Plan and Achieve Your Goals.* 2d ed. New York: AMACOM Books, 2008.

Rouillard, Larrie. *Crisp: Goals and Goal Setting: Achieving Measured Objectives.* 3d ed. Florence, Ky.: Crisp Learning, 2002.

Business goals aren't that much different from personal goals. For example, a manager may say, "This year we'll improve our corporate image, land new accounts from big investors, increase profits, and cut costs."

A goal is an end one strives to attain. The clearer your vision of the end, the better shot you have of reaching it.

Goals define our mission in life. Without goals we have no direction, and without direction, we have no criteria to judge.

—Amy Lindgren, president and founder of Prototype Career Services

GOAL VISUALIZATION

Visualization is the practice of envisioning and maintaining a mental picture. Visualizing your goal means you picture what things will look like when you've achieved your goal.

Barry, now a successful sales manager, says he learned the art of visualization from his high-school basketball coach. "I had problems with my foul shot. So Coach had me stand at the line, get set for the shot, then try to picture myself shooting the ball and catching nothing but net. We did it in practice. Then right before I took a foul shot in a game, I always visualized the ball going in."

Whether it's sinking a foul shot or delivering a presentation, visualizing your goal can help you accomplish it. (Chet Gordon, The Image Works)

Everything you can imagine is real.

—Pablo Picasso, artist

When Barry joined his sales team, he applied his visualization technique. "The first time I had to give a big presentation, I was really nervous. So I kept picturing myself standing up, pointing at the graphs, and sounding confident. It put me at ease."

Visualization is more than just a mental trick. If you can't see clearly to the end of the line, chances are your goal lacks clarity.

TYPES OF GOALS

Good goals are specific and definable.

Talking about goals can get confusing. We can talk about *long-range goals* and *short-range goals.* Your desire to be a forest ranger when you grow up could be considered a long-range goal. Your desire to make the soccer team next month is a relatively short-term goal.

Your company may have a general, humanitarian goal of serving the community or fostering understanding. But your business goals are much more focused. Good goals are specific and definable. Otherwise, you'll never know if you reach them.

For example, let's go back to your New Year's resolutions. If your goal is to lose weight, how will you know for sure when you've succeeded? Have you completed your goal as soon as you lose one ounce or 50 pounds?

Most businesses aim to increase their profits. But the stuffed-bear manufacturer discussed in Chapter 5

DOS AND DON'TS OF SETTING GOALS

DO	DON'T
Get to the root cause.	Settle for the effect.
Be specific.	Be general.
Relate the goal to the overall purpose.	Be uninformed.
Include a time frame.	Make a wish and hope for the best.
Visualize the result.	Lump goals and objectives together.

will have a more useful goal if it's specific, such as "Maintain overhead costs at current level, but increase the quality of stuffed bears by 10 percent." Now the company can visualize the results: better quality, more profit.

GET REAL

For a goal to be workable and helpful, it has to be specific. However, it also needs to be realistic. What happens to your New Year's resolutions when you set your goals too high? Perhaps you set a goal to lose 60 pounds and date the most popular senior in

Go ahead and dream the impossible dream, but when you write down your goals, be realistic.

Never try to solve all the problems at once—make them line up for you one-by-one.

—Richard Sloma, attorney and lecturer

high school. Chances are you'll get discouraged early on because you know there's no way to guarantee you'll reach that goal. Even if you lose 20 pounds and have a decent date for homecoming, you're still not satisfied.

Goals must be attainable. Companies have to do research before they set their goals. They can't just wish a figure and hope for the best. Go ahead and dream the impossible dream, but when you write down your goals, be realistic.

☞ FACT

According to the Small Business Administration, approximately 97 percent of the population fails to set goals for two reasons: FEAR (which stands for false evidence appearing real) and the risk involved if the goal is not reached.

SETTING OBJECTIVES

In most cases, *objectives* are bite-sized, measurable goals that will lead to the fulfillment of an overall goal. Say you decide your goal is to lose 10 pounds by June 1—the date the swimming pool opens.

You've made your goal specific and measurable and given yourself a reasonable time frame.

Now it's time to break that goal into smaller steps, or objectives. Each objective should be measurable, so you'll know if you've reached it. Perhaps you settle on losing half a pound a week. You'll weigh your-

OBJECTIVES FOR WRITING AN "A" TERM PAPER

Goal: To research, write, and turn in an "A" term paper by March 16th.

Objective: Brainstorm 20 topics and select one by February 1st.

Objective: Draft thesis by February 3rd.

Objective: Complete general library research by February 10th.

Objective: Complete outline by February 15th.

Objective: Complete specific research by February 25th.

Objective: Write the first draft of paper by March 1st.

Objective: Write the second draft by March 7th.

Objective: Type and proofread final draft by March 14th.

self weekly and keep a record in a little book by the scale. How are you going to accomplish this goal?

First, you will exercise five days a week for 30 minutes at a time. Next, you need to change your eating habits. You make an objective to read three cookbooks on low-fat recipes. You'll pack your lunch and make your own dinners and breakfasts. You continue with your objectives until you're confident that fulfilling each objective will lead you to your goal. By the

✍ EXERCISE

1. Circle the specific goals. Rewrite the more general goals to make them specific (and as a result, more effective).

    • Our company will improve its corporate image.

    • I'll get Tom to take me to a movie by the end of this month.

    • Our department will increase sales by 10 percent this year.

    • The company will downsize 25 percent of its personnel, with no more than a 10-percent loss in productivity.

    • This year I'll become popular.

2. Choose one of the specific goals you've created above and list at least five objectives under it.

time you pull on that swimsuit, you'll be 10 pounds thinner.

You may have to research each objective. Will losing half a pound a week bring you to your goal? How much exercise do you require to lose weight? What exercises are best for your objective?

Good objectives usually combine a measurable end with an action and a time frame. Objectives are like footprints leading to a treasure: If you follow each step, you should end up at the treasure. If you miss a step or veer off track, you won't get there. All you have to do to reach your goal is reach each objective along the way. But how do you reach those objectives? Read on.

✔ TRUE OR FALSE: ANSWERS

Do You Know How to Define Goals and Objectives?

1. It's important to set realistic goals.

True. It's okay to dream big, but do your research before setting a goal to ensure that you won't be disappointed if you can't reach it. For example, you don't want to set a goal of increasing quarterly profits by 35 percent if you know there's no way—no matter how hard you work—that you will be able to do so. Doing this will just raise your employer's expectations and most likely result in disappointment when you're unable to reach the goal.

2. Visualization is an excellent tool to help you reach your goals.

True. Visualization, in which you anticipate the positive achievement of your goal, will work for almost anyone—from a student preparing to give a speech in class to a professional baseball player imagining that he'll get a clutch hit to win a game.

3. Establishing objectives will help you meet your goals.

True. Sometimes when we establish goals, they seem big and unattainable. Objectives are mini-goals (like a step on a ladder) that will help you gradually reach the ultimate goal. When setting goals, it's important to establish a series of measurable goals (with deadlines) that will help you along in the process.

IN SUMMARY . . .

- In order to be effective, solutions must be connected to the root of a problem.

- Goals need to be both specific and attainable.

- Visualizing the desired result is a good way to set a goal and achieve it.

- Objectives are small steps that lead directly to a goal.

7

STEP 3—
GENERATE
SOLUTIONS

*Nature operates by profusion. Think of the nearly
infinite number of seeds that fall to earth, only a
fraction of which take root to become trees; . . . of the
millions of sperm competing so fiercely to fertilize one
small egg. Similarly, human beings engaged in the
creative process explore an astronomical number of
possible patterns before settling on an idea.*

—Gabriele Lusser Rico in *Writing the Natural Way*

You've identified and defined the problem. You've
drawn up specific goals and objectives. Now you
need to decide how to meet those objectives. Take
that term paper you scheduled in the last chapter.
The goals and objectives for it are in place. You now
have time limits and measurable outcomes.

But what will you write about? Now it's time to
generate ideas—lots of ideas. The more choices you

Do You Know How to Generate Solutions to Problems?

1. Brainstorming is only for creative people.

2. It's important to keep an open mind regarding teammates' ideas during the brainstorming process.

3. Freewriting is a waste of time. It never helps me generate any ideas.

Test yourself as you read through this chapter. The answers appear on pages 124–125.

give yourself—the more possible solutions—the better your final selection will be.

Want to write on dinosaurs? There's a good chance that your paper will be boring and not distinguished from everyone else's if you choose the first idea that comes to you. Instead, think of 10, 20, even 50 possible topics so you can end up with a winning topic.

MULTIPLE CHOICES

Are you one of those people who never feel creative? Perhaps you feel that you lack originality and that you're just not the creative type. Creativity and originality are essentials for any problem solver, and your employer will expect you to bring a degree of creativity to your work.

Don't panic. Creativity is within your reach if you're willing to practice coming up with multiple choices. Learn to generate lots of ideas.

Not long ago, *Teen Magazine* decided to change its image. They wanted to reach older, more mature teens. When goals and objectives were set, the magazine hired public-relations consultants to come up with possible ways the magazine might change its image.

A member of the public-relations team explains what happened next. "We met as a team to come up with ideas. It was rather like a game show, where contestants had to spout off as many words or phrases as they could think of in five minutes."

They listed possible changes, like lipstick and lipstick colors, tone of writing, color of cover, models for cover, inside art, features, headings and graphics, products advertised, and so on. "At the end of five minutes, the four of us had about 120 ideas. We had a lot to choose from."

That's what you want at this stage of problem solving: multiple choices. Brainstorming is the best way to get them.

The creative person wants to be a know-it-all. He wants to know about all kinds of things—ancient

history, 19th-century mathematics, current manu-
facturing techniques, flower arranging, and hog
futures—because he never knows when these ideas
might come together to form a new idea. It may
happen six minutes later or six months, or six years
down the road. But he has faith that it will happen.

—Carl Ally, American advertising copywriter

BRAINSTORMING

Brainstorming is the practice of quickly generating multiple ideas without restraining the free flow of possible solutions. Katie brainstormed her way through high school and college and straight onto a team of researchers in the Southwest. She explains, "In high school, brainstorming was how we raised money for projects, came up with group ideas, and decided on science fair projects. I brainstormed big assignments so I'd have several ideas in case one didn't work out. It's the same technique we use where I work to solve every problem we run into."

Chapter 2 discussed right brain/left brain thinking. In a way, your right brain holds the inspired ideas, those crazy notions that just might be what your work team is looking for. But your left brain, rational and logical, realizes how bizarre the right brain ideas can get. So the reliable left brain jumps in and censors that bright idea before it comes out.

Does this confirm what you've always suspected—that you do have a split personality? Not really. You

*Brainstorming is a great way to quickly generate many ideas—
especially those that your rational mind might not normally consider.*
(Jim Craigmyle, Corbis)

just have two distinct kinds of thinking going on at
the same time.

Brainstorming is designed to get those great, sometimes hidden, ideas out before you squelch them. In
order for the process to work, you need to follow a
few ground rules.

Set a Time Limit
If you're brainstorming a topic for your term paper
or an invention to make you a millionaire, you'll
have better luck brainstorming ideas for five focused

minutes than you will trying to come up with some-thing for five hours. Set a time limit. Get out all the right-brain ideas as fast as you can. After a few minutes, your left brain will step in and take over anyway.

When you're in a group brainstorming session, your team might want to set a time limit—say, 10 minutes—for pure brainstorming. Then you can step back and see what you've come up with.

Don't Judge Your Teammates

If it's so hard to get these fresh, original (and some-times bizarre) ideas out to us, imagine working at problem solving with a team. Each member of your

DOS AND DON'TS OF BRAINSTORMING SESSIONS

DO	DON'T
Speak/write quickly.	Think too hard.
Say the first thing that comes to mind.	Censure yourself.
Be open to all suggestions.	Analyze.
Respect every idea.	Slow down.

work team needs to abide by this ground rule: No judgments should be made during brainstorming.

If team members feel their ideas are going to be evaluated as soon as they say them, that may very well be the end of their contribution to the brainstorming session. They will censure themselves before anyone else gets a chance, and that censured solution may be the one you need.

Trust has to exist in a team brainstorming session, or the best solutions may be stifled before they leave the right brain.

Abide by this ground rule: No judgments should be made during brainstorming.

Every Idea Has Merit

After all the ideas are out in the open, the team should generate a long list of possible solutions. Every idea is worth recording.

It's time to see what you've come up with. Instead of heading straight for the two or three ideas that sound best, a great problem solver will keep this rule in mind: Every idea has merit. Great problem solvers look at every idea, no matter how bizarre it may be. Some of the best solutions come as a result of piecing together bits of several seemingly implausible solutions.

Imagine your problem is that you're failing history. Your goal is to get a B by the end of the semester. You put together objectives and a time frame. Then you brainstorm, following all the ground rules.

First, you turn off the MP3 player and TV and lock your door. Now you're ready to try a method of brainstorming called listing. With your desk cleared, sit with paper and pen, ready to write down every possible solution that comes to you for getting a B in history.

- Meet teacher
- Ask Mom and Dad for help
- Study with X, Y, and/or Z
- Cheat
- Go to counseling
- Read outside books
- Ask for extra credit
- Study my old tests
- Get a tutor
- Beg teacher for a B
- Take speed reading
- Transfer
- Find last year's final
- Study one hour a night

When five minutes are up, you put your pen down. At first glance, you may want to laugh at some of your ideas. But you've vowed to consider every idea. For example, you can't cheat and copy Smart Sally's test. But you can call Sally and ask if you may look at her last five quizzes so you can correct your paper and have the right answers to study for the final.

You know it won't do any good to beg your teacher to give you a B. But you might ask what you need to do in order to bring your grade up to a B.

Brainstorming can help you with problems ranging from a topic for your term paper, a gift for your boyfriend, a restaurant to take your girlfriend, or what your employer should do to increase profits. Practice the art of brainstorming. The ability to come up with multiple solutions will give you a reputation as a good problem solver.

BRAINSTORMING TECHNIQUES

Listing is only one method of brainstorming. Working with a team of problem solvers and calling out ideas as they come to you is another method. Many other techniques of brainstorming can be used to unleash right-brain thoughts before the left brain has a chance to censor them.

Some of these methods will work for you; others won't. Use them as tools. Store the techniques in your mental toolbox, a bag of tricks you can pull out when you need them to help you fix problems.

Word Association

You've heard about word associations that psychiatrists use. You've probably played a game built on word associations. For example, one person says to another, "When I say a word, give me the first word

ANOTHER BENEFIT OF BRAINSTORMING

Brainstorming doesn't just help you solve problems, it can also earn you $5,000. The Henkel Corporation, a manufacturer of duct-tape, awards this amount to someone who submits the best story about how he or she used duct-tape in an innovative way. Some of the more interesting uses for duct-tape detailed by past contest participants include using it to help set a broken ankle, remove warts, repair a damaged airplane, fix a pair of split pants in an emergency, and temporarily repair a flat tire. Visit http://www.duck tapeclub.com for more information on the contest and the many uses for duct-tape.

that comes into your mind. *Love.*" The other person then says the first thing that comes to mind, without thinking about it. Your uninhibited answers to such questions will tell a lot about you. If your answer surprises even you, your right brain slipped one past the more orderly left brain. And that's the idea.

How can this help you solve a problem at work? Imagine that your boss wants your work team to come up with a new motto, a slogan for your prod-

HELPFUL BOOKS ON BRAINSTORMING

Clegg, Brian, and Paul Birch. *Instant Creativity: Simple Techniques to Ignite Innovation & Problem Solving.* London, U.K.: Kogan Page, 2007.

Cory, Timothy R., and Thomas Slater. *Brainstorming: Techniques for New Ideas.* Bloomington, Ind.: iUniverse, 2003.

Foster, Jack, and Larry Corby. *How to Get Ideas.* 2d ed. San Francisco: Berrett-Koehler Publishers, 2007.

Harrison, Sam. *IdeaSpotting: How to Find Your Next Great Idea.* Cincinnati, Ohio: How Books, 2006.

Michalko, Michael. *Thinkpak: A Brainstorming Card Deck.* Rev. ed. Berkeley, Calif.: Ten Speed Press, 2006.

Monahan, Tom. *The Do It Yourself Lobotomy: Open Your Mind to Greater Creative Thinking.* Hoboken, N.J.: Wiley, 2002.

Rich, Jason. *Brain Storm: Tap Into Your Creativity to Generate Awesome Ideas and Remarkable Results.* Franklin Lakes, N.J.: Career Press, 2003.

Ries, Estelle H. *How to Get Ideas.* Whitefish, Mont.: Kessinger Publishing, LLC, 2007.

Souter, Nick. *Creative Business Solutions: Breakthrough Thinking: Brainstorming for Inspiration and Ideas.* New York: Sterling Publishing, 2007.

uct, a cleanser called "Green Clean." One way to generate ideas is to take each word in the product name and apply word association. You can ask a coworker, "What's the first thing that comes into your mind when I say green?"

Some responses might be, "Spring." "Pasture." "Lime." "New." "Inexperienced."

Now do the same kind of word association with "Clean." Here your coworker might respond with, "House." "Fresh." "Maid."

Using all of these responses, you can develop a potential slogan: "Use Green Clean and bring springtime to your house." While this slogan may not be the one your boss chooses, you can always brainstorm again to come up with another one.

Clustering or Mapping

Clustering, like free-word association, is a brainstorming technique to help you spill out flashes of inspiration in unplanned relationships. Thoughts come out as clusters.

In clustering, you write a trigger word in the center of your paper. Circle the word. Then, as fast as you can, write the words or ideas that pop into your head. Circle each word and connect word balloons that come together. When that thought process slows, start another chain of word balloons.

The cluster of ideas on the next page focuses on possible directions for a magazine to take on a wedding issue. When you finish the cluster, look it over

carefully—not just for words, but for the clusters, the relationships between words. You may have released a complex design or connection you can put to good use.

Starbursting

Starbursting "is a form of brainstorming that focuses on generating questions rather than answers," according to Mind Tools. For example, if a work team is brainstorming a new type of electric shaver, members will create a series of questions about the product to spotlight any potential weaknesses.

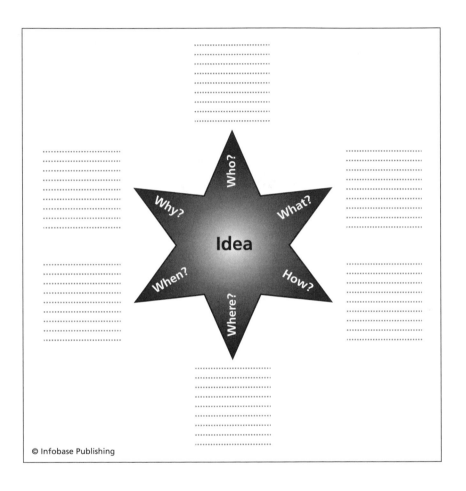

These might include: "What makes the razor different than the ones already on the market?"; "What are its new features?"; "Who is the intended audience? Young men? Older men with especially heavy beards?"; "Why would these people buy it?"; "How will we market the product? Television? Internet? Print media?"; "How much will it cost?"; "When will it be ready to sell?" Answers to these questions should lead to even more detailed questions until all aspects of the razor—from design and production to advertising—are covered.

Starbursting is a good way to understand a new product, service, or idea, and get the kinks out before it is created or implemented.

Freewriting

Your English teacher may have introduced you to freewriting. "Class, everybody write whatever comes into your mind for five minutes." Although it may sound like permission to scribble, freewriting can be an effective brainstorming technique if your mind is stuck on a problem.

Cari wrestled with a customer-service problem the first year she worked for an international airline. She explains how freewriting helped her come up with a needed solution. "It was the first time a customer had complained that I wasn't helpful. Her problem was that she didn't have the frequent-flyer mileage to get the prize she wanted. That's what I told her, but she wanted more."

Cari took five minutes away from the phones while the customer talked to her supervisor. "I just started writing the first thing that came into my head—that the woman was a nutcase, I hated my job, etc. Then I started writing out her options. She could get a partial ticket to St. Louis, have the mileage she needed, and get her upgrade on that."

SURF THE WEB: BRAINSTORMING WEBSITES

Brainstorming
http://www.unc.edu/depts/wcweb/handouts/
brainstorming.html

Brainstorming.co.uk
http://www.brainstorming.co.uk/contents.html

EffectiveMeetings.com
http://www.effectivemeetings.com

Empowersu.com
http://www.empowersu.com/articles/
motivational/brainstorming-review.html

Mind Tools: Brainstorming
http://www.mindtools.com/brainstm.html

Cari quickly jotted down the solution and passed it to her supervisor. Her quick thinking didn't go unnoticed. An account of that incident went into her folder and helped get her high marks on her first evaluation.

Freewriting can be completely freewheeling, or it can be guided. Instead of writing down whatever came to her head, Cari might have started out by focusing on the customer's options. But as her story shows, both methods can help bring your best ideas to the surface.

✍ EXERCISE

1. Brainstorm for five minutes and try to come up with as many solutions as possible for the following situations:

   - It's time to turn in your three-page test, but you're out of staples. How can you get the pages to stay together?

   - Your new concoction, The Marshmallow Puff bar, isn't selling well at your school. How can you get students at your school to spend their money on your candy bar instead of on a Snickers or Kit Kat bar?

   - You're driving to a friend's party in another town, but realize that you've forgotten the directions. How can you get to the party without having to go all the away home to retrieve the directions?

   - You're locked out of your house. How do you get back in without a key or get a key?

   - You start baking a cake, but realize you don't have any butter on hand and all the stores are closed. What can you do to finish the cake?

2. Try clustering the following words to see what you come up with:

   - success

   - failure

   - hate

   - friendship

When you freewrite, it's important to keep writing even if you think that you're creating gibberish. Insights lurk amidst the gibberish and nonsense. Highlight these words or phrases and write them on a separate sheet of paper, then study them until you begin to see ideas emerge. Once you've generated more ideas, conduct another freewriting session to explore the concepts further.

Now that you're loaded with ways to come up with possible solutions, it's time for a plan of action.

✔ TRUE OR FALSE: ANSWERS

Do You Know How to Generate Solutions to Problems?

1. Brainstorming is only for creative people.

False. First of all, everyone has a creative side—they just need to open themselves up to this type of thinking. Second, brainstorming—via its many techniques—is an effective tool for anyone who wants to solve a problem. Even the most scientific-oriented thinkers have a creative side that helps them generate ideas and solve problems.

2. It's important to keep an open mind regarding teammates' ideas during the brainstorming process.

True. You should always treat your coworkers with respect—plus, you never know where a good idea will come from. Perhaps a coworker will suggest something that might inspire you to come up with an even better idea.

3. Freewriting is a waste of time. It never helps me generate any ideas.

False. It may feel like it sometimes, but if you really embrace freewriting, you'll be surprised at how it eventually will help you generate ideas and allow you to think about problems from different angles.

IN SUMMARY . . .

- To brainstorm effectively, don't immediately discount anything. All ideas are worth writing down.

- Do not make judgments about your teammates when brainstorming. Every person should be allowed to give his or her ideas in an uninhibited way.

- Word association may allow your right brain to momentarily conquer your more sensible left brain. This type of uninhibited thought helps in brainstorming.

- When you finish coming up with a cluster of ideas, be sure to pay attention to the relationships between words—you may have actually come up with a complex design.

- Starbursting is a unique way of generating solutions because it uses questions to spotlight potential weaknesses in products, ideas, and services before they are actually created or implemented.

- Freewriting can be guided or unguided. It is a good technique for bringing ideas to the surface.

8

STEP 4—DEVELOP A PLAN OF ACTION

If you're following these simple problem-solving steps, you should have many possible solutions to your problem. Now all you have to do is decide which solution is the pick of the litter.

Even if you're on the right track, you'll get run over if you just sit there.

—Will Rogers, American humorist

EVALUATING CHOICES

Remember how important it is in the previous step to not be judgmental? You don't want to hamper the free flow of ideas and possibilities. You keep that analytical, critical side of yourself at bay so that you can come up with as many problem-solving choices as possible.

✔ TRUE OR FALSE?

Do You Have a Plan of Action?

1. It's okay to have more than one plan of action when solving a problem.

2. When delegating assignments, the project leader should just put all the assignments in a hat and let workers pick a task.

3. As a rookie on a problem-solving team, it's important to be a team player, show initiative, and be willing to take on the least glamorous jobs.

Test yourself as you read through this chapter. The answers appear on pages 138–139.

Now it's time to analyze your choices and formulate an action plan. Whereas the previous step requires the creative powers of right-brain thinking, choosing a plan of action requires all the logical powers residing in your left brain.

When Brad started working for a solar-panel company in Hawaii, he thought he'd found his dream job. And what job could be more secure than selling solar panels in a location with so much sun!

But right away, Brad saw he was wrong. His company was actually in danger of going under. He had been hired in hopes that he might shed a new perspective on his team's problems. Brad's boss handed him a file of possible solutions they had considered. Did they need a better product? Better salespeople? A new location? More advertising? What could they do to attract enough customers?

Brad studied the data gathered on every conceivable answer. His team had already determined the root problem. They had a great product, super location, experienced salespeople, and a hefty advertising budget. The problem was the way Hawaiians viewed solar-panel companies in general. Most companies had reputations as being fly-by-night businesses.

Brad was closer to a solution, but he still had choices to evaluate. He and the rest of the team brainstormed about more ideas for establishing the company's positive image.

As Brad evaluated their choices, he narrowed the possibilities to two:

1. Conduct an ad campaign to convince people their company was not one of the fly-by-nighters.

2. Make a positive image for the company through an all-new campaign.

In evaluating these final options, Brad gathered more data and statistics. He interviewed potential customers. He studied what similar companies had done and what had failed. At last, Brad was ready with his recommendation for an action plan.

Once Alexander Graham Bell came up with the idea for the telephone, he had to carefully develop a plan of action to take the concept from idea to finished product. (Scherl/SV-Bilderdienst, The Image Works)

☞ FACT

When Alexander Graham Bell faced the problem of how the human voice might be carried over great distances, his solution was the telephone. But how did he follow through with his invention? Although Bell was an expert in sound, he knew little about electricity. Before he could build a model of his machine, he had to study and learn about electricity. Then he could begin applying his knowledge and creativity to solving technical problems.

MODIFY AND SELECT A PLAN OF ACTION

Use your powers of analytical thought to evaluate each possible solution. Investigate each one rigorously, but the time will come to make up your mind. You may modify one solution or combine two or more possible solutions, but you need to settle on one plan of action.

Brad's final recommendation for his solar-panel company was to begin a vigorous, positive, all-new ad campaign. Trying to explain themselves to the public would only link them with fly-by-night businesses. Brad suggested they proceed as if people already believed in them. He drew up a plan of action.

LIST STEPS IN YOUR PLAN OF ACTION

Once the solution is settled on, everyone should set to work on detailing the plan. Here's where you need your skills at setting goals and objectives. Break down the larger goal (to change the company's image by next year) into smaller goals and objectives.

As soon as Brad and his solar-panel company settled on their plan of action—to conduct a statewide positive image campaign over the next 12 months—they got down to business. A step-by-step strategy targeted all local media. Their own materials and flyers were rewritten. Salespeople were called in for seminars on projecting confidence and the right image.

Over the next year, Brad developed ads in which he referred to his company as "the Sunshine Guys." They had their own jingle, their own success stories, and their own emblem. Eventually, the whole island

A PLAN OF ACTION INCLUDES . . .

- a clear statement of the overall plan

- goals and clear-cut objectives

- a step-by-step strategy

- a schedule with deadlines

- allocation of human and financial resources

- delegation of jobs

- contingency plans

- an internal review system

could sing their jingle and grew to trust the Sunshine Guys. The bold plan of action had set Brad's company apart from their competitors.

ESTABLISH A SCHEDULE

A time line of action is an integral part of forming a plan of action. When will new brochures need to be issued? March 15? That means the rewritten copy must be completed by . . . which means the writer or publicity firm must be hired by . . . . Scheduling needs to be specific and realistic, encompassing every part of the action plan.

Each objective should have its own deadline or deadlines. And those deadlines have to be coordinated with all other objectives. In Brad's solar-panel campaign in Hawaii, his coworkers and he decided on a media blitz, with print, radio, and television advertising starting the same day. In this type of campaign, Brad and his coworkers have a number of individuals to contact and coordinate with. They must consider the importance of each contact and plan all of the schedules accordingly.

One of the worst crimes a team member can commit against his team is to miss a deadline. Don't do it. Your geography teacher may have been understanding of missed deadlines, but your team can't afford this luxury. If you fail to meet your deadline, you could single-handedly derail your company's action plan.

As a manager of a small editorial staff that produces dozens of textbooks each year, it is extremely important to know the strengths and weaknesses of each of my staff members. Some are better at proofreading or product development, while others excel at writing and page layout. Knowing each individual's strengths allows me to assign the appropriate task to the appropriate worker—thereby ensuring that production deadlines are met and quality publications are created.

—George Sell, managing editor, book publishing company

DELEGATING

Once all the individual parts of the plan of action have been detailed, with goals and objectives in place and a time line established, it's time to delegate the work, deciding who does what. A good manager or team leader will delegate wisely. Work should be as evenly distributed as possible. And team members should be working in areas of their strengths.

I not only use all the brains I have, but all I can borrow.

—Woodrow Wilson, U.S. president

As the rookie on the problem-solving team, you may not get the jobs you want. The team may put

DOS AND DON'TS OF A GOOD PROBLEM-SOLVING TEAM

DO	DON'T
Delegate responsibilities.	Make one person do all of the work.
Specify goals and work toward them as a team.	Have different goals.
Establish a timeline and make sure that everyone on the team knows it.	Plan last-minute tasks without letting everyone know about them.
Brainstorm together to get everyone's ideas on the table.	Quickly draw up a plan without thinking it through.
Encourage people to speak freely.	Judge your teammates and make them feel inhibited.

you in charge of copying materials, when all you want is a crack at creating television ads. Realize that you're going to have to earn those glitzier jobs.

Give all you've got to whatever assignments you are given. Then you may do better next time.

If you get to volunteer for tasks, don't just ask for the more glamorous or the easier jobs. Everybody will know why your hand went up, and your coworkers won't appreciate it. Instead, volunteer for tasks you know you can do well. Communicate effectively, asking what's involved in the task and being honest about your strengths and weaknesses. Ask for the legwork jobs that nobody wants. Do more than you have to do just to hold up your end.

Don't consider your job done when you've accomplished everything you've been delegated. You're not done until the whole plan is accomplished. So if you find yourself with free time on your hands, ask your teammates what you can do to help them with their responsibilities.

Hold yourself responsible for a higher standard than anybody else expects of you.

—Henry Ward Beecher, American clergyman

PUTTING IT ALL TOGETHER

A sound action plan includes other essentials, too. How much money will you need to see the plan through? Where will you get the funds? Will you need more personnel? More space? More direction?

✍ EXERCISE

Draw up your own plan of action for successfully getting into the right college.

- Brainstorm your possibilities. (Where and
  how?)

- Evaluate your choices. (You could play
  lots of video games, or you could study
  to get good grades. You could fill out
  scholarship applications, or you could
  just watch movies instead.)

- Modify and select a plan. (State it clearly
  in writing.)

- List the steps you'll need to pull off your
  plan. (Fill out applications; get your
  transcripts sent, etc.)

- Schedule the preceding steps. (Give
  yourself a deadline for completing the
  applications.)

- Delegate. (Have your family help with
  college research or ask around to find
  out which colleges
  are the best for your interests.)

- Put it together. (Go ahead and do it.)

The way to achieve success is first to have a definite, clear, practical idea—a goal or an objective. Second, have the necessary means to achieve your ends— wisdom, money, materials, methods. Third, adjust all your means to that end.

—Aristotle, Greek philosopher

Every great Plan A has a good Plan B waiting in the wings—just in case. Chapter 9 deals with contingency plans and troubleshooting.

✔ TRUE OR FALSE: ANSWERS

Do You Have a Plan of Action?

1. It's okay to have more than one plan of action when solving a problem.

False. You need to choose one plan; otherwise, your team may end up focusing on conflicting approaches. It's okay if you combine two of the final ideas if they both are strong and complementary, but stick to one plan of action.

2. When delegating assignments, the project leader should just put all the assignments in a hat and let workers pick a task.

False. A good project leader knows the strengths and weaknesses of his or her workers—and assigns tasks based on their strengths and abilities. Additionally, a good leader evenly distributes work assignments so that no one feels overwhelmed.

3. As a rookie on a problem-solving team, it's important to be a team player, show initiative, and be willing to take on the least glamorous jobs.

True. Doing these things will make you a valued member of the team, and hopefully help you to gain more responsibility for future projects.

IN SUMMARY . . .

- Make sure that your plan of action includes delegating responsibilities. If multiple people work on something, it will likely get done faster.

- Realize that you will have to climb your way up the ladder at work. Do more than is expected of you, and you will eventually be given more responsibility.

- Evaluate your choices carefully and remember to keep the overall outcome in mind.

- Write a time line that specifically states your plan. Stick to the dates on this time line religiously—this is the only way you will ever complete things on time.

- Don't forget to specify exactly what will be necessary to complete a task. Think over even such small details as who will purchase supplies and provide transportation.

9

STEP 5—FOLLOW THROUGH

Don't forget
about the follow-
through step.

You've done it! You've gone from a brainstorming session of wild ideas, through research and analysis, to come up with a plan of action. You've broken that plan into detailed steps with deadlines. Assignments have been delegated, and your team is ready to charge.

But hold on just a minute. Don't forget about the follow-through step. The best time to begin follow through is before you start.

If anything can go wrong, it will.

—Murphy's Law

ANTICIPATE PROBLEMS

Before you and your team race out of the conference room and head separate ways, anticipate potential problems with your plan. Try a variation

140

✔ TRUE OR FALSE?

Are You Ready to Follow Through?

1. When creating a plan to solve a problem, it's important to develop a contingency plan in case your original plan hits a roadblock.

2. Good teams troubleshoot problems ahead of time.

3. There is no need to celebrate the accomplishment of goals. Just meeting them is enough of a reward.

Test yourself as you read through this chapter. The answers appear on pages 153–154.

on a brainstorming session. Ask, "What could go wrong?"

People don't always react the way you think they will. If your plan hinges on certain people, ask what-if questions. "What if she's too angry to say yes?" "What if he won't see us?" "What if her schedule is full or she doesn't like the plan?"

Money never goes quite as far as you think it will. What if you run out of money in your ad campaign? Might the radio have raised its commercial rate? And what if you get into the campaign and see it's not working?

Should you ask for more help, just in case? Do you have enough access to the copy machine? And what if the city has another blackout? Always anticipate potential problems.

However, no amount of planning can predict everything. As analytical and logical as our left brain may be, it's not all-knowing. But if we can anticipate what might go wrong, we'll be better prepared and likely less frustrated when things do go wrong.

Jerry works for a large trucking company, supplying rigs to clients. He does all he can to anticipate possible problems for his customers. "Anticipating trouble is the easiest part of my job. I helped raise my six younger brothers and sisters. Something was always bound to go wrong." He explains that he feels it's part of his duty to prepare his customers for unforeseen trouble. "I check the weather and try to let them know if that might slow delivery. I always tell them somebody might return the rig late to us, or it might need repair. Then if something happens, they remember I warned them, and they're not quite so upset."

DEVELOP A CONTINGENCY PLAN

A *contingency* is something that depends on unforeseen or accidental occurrences. You do all you can to make sure your plan of action will succeed. But just in case it doesn't, it's a good idea to plan for any contingency. If Plan A falls apart, do you have a Plan B?

If you worked through the problem-solving process, you do have contingency plans. When you generated all those possible solutions and evaluated their worth, you left behind several alternative plans. So before you start Plan A, make sure you select a Plan B to keep on the back burner. If you are fortunate, you'll never need it. But if you do need it, you'll be glad it's there waiting for you.

Tess directed a nursing home in a major city. Although it was located in a densely populated area, the number of patients were declining and so were operating funds. The administrative team decided to raise money and at the same time get neighborhood residents in for a visit. If residents could see for themselves the quality of the common areas and rooms and the professionalism of the workers, the staff believed the problem would be solved.

Tess and her staff organized a community rummage and yard sale at the nursing home. They hoped to raise a little cash. More important, neighbors could have the chance to check out the nursing home.

All went according to Tess's well-thought-out plans, except for one unforeseen problem. Neighbors poured into the yard sale, but nobody ventured inside the nursing home. Then Tess remembered one of the plans they had rejected in favor of the yard sale. One of the staff members had suggested that they hold the show inside the nursing home.

Tess had her staff bring all of the assorted sales items inside. Now visitors had to go inside to see the merchandise. Once inside, many neighbors took a tour of the home and talked with staff members. Some even asked for more information on the nursing home's services and facilities. Tess was grateful for the contingency plan.

TROUBLESHOOTING

Competent teams try to trouble-shoot problems before they arise.

Troubleshooting means investigating, finding, and eliminating the source of trouble. Most troubleshooting occurs when a plan runs into real problems. But competent teams try to troubleshoot problems before they arise.

How can you troubleshoot a problem ahead of time? Take a test run. Try your strategy on a small warm-up audience. Jay Leno has a habit of trying out his jokes and monologue material at a small nightclub before delivering them on the *Tonight Show*. If the joke bombs in the test audience, he may have saved himself a big embarrassment on national television. He can "fix" the joke or throw it out altogether.

If at all possible, try your plan out before you commit all the troops. Then alter the plan before it's too late.

BE FLEXIBLE WHEN CONFRONTED WITH PROBLEMS

Anticipate potential problems. Make contingency plans. Troubleshoot your ideas. But no matter how thorough you are, you'll run into problems. Be flexible when you encounter them.

_____

Poor thinkers judge too quickly and uncritically, ignoring the need for evidence and letting their feelings shape their conclusions. Blind to their limitations and predispositions, poor thinkers trust their judgment implicitly, ignoring the possibility of imperfections, complications, or negative responses.

—Vincent Ryan Ruggiero in *The Art of Thinking*

Flexibility is highly valued in a problem solver. Flexibility is an asset because even top dollar can't buy omniscience. Movie advertisers put together a short film clip, or trailer, to promote movies. The clip includes quick scenes or snatches of dialogue from the actual movie, a slogan or catchphrase ("Be afraid. Be very afraid.") or staged testimonials ("I was so scared, I spilled my popcorn!").

But regardless of the money producers put into these trailers, the ad people can miss the mark. So producers and ad people have to be flexible. If marketing surveys indicate that no one is buying this future film as a scary movie, the advertisers pick a different clip, call it the greatest love story ever told, and run a new trailer.

You may not have the resources to put together a whole new campaign. But you owe your employer and your coworkers flexibility. When you run into a brick wall, you can crumble into pieces, or you can flex and find a way around it.

BE PERSISTENT TO MEET GOALS AND COMPLETE PROJECTS

Remember, we're talking about solving a problem, a real problem. Your job as a problem solver isn't finished when you get your grand action plan. Your job isn't over until the problem is solved.

Some men give up their designs when they almost reach their goals; while others, on the contrary, obtain a victory by exerting, at the last moment, more vigorous efforts than before.

—Polybius, Greek historian

Each person on your team should persist in the completion of every objective. If some director won't talk to you on the phone, show up in person. If that doesn't work, send a telegram, flowers, or a chocolate chip cookie. Persist. Don't stop until you get what you want.

Keep in mind that vision of the end. Remember why you started in the first place. It takes persistence to stay with a plan until it's completed.

✍ EXERCISE

The following are examples of worst-case scenarios. Put yourself in the shoes of the person involved in each scenario. What type of Plan B would you have developed beforehand to eliminate these disasters?

- You are employed as a wedding planner, and the outdoor wedding you've so carefully organized is being drenched by rain.

- Several of the foreign acts you booked for your school's international music fest cancel at the last minute because of an airline strike.

- Your college application to Harvard is rejected.

- The apartment you planned to rent was given to somebody else.

- You are making a PowerPoint presentation to a large group of people when your computer freezes.

Plan B Solutions

- You might have erected a large tent near the wedding grounds as a backup, or you could have reserved space at a nearby hall or auditorium as a contingency plan.

- You might have gathered a list of local musicians interested in filling in at the last minute in the event of a cancellation.

(continues)

(continued)

- You would have avoided putting yourself into a corner by applying to at least five colleges with a variety of admission requirements.

- You might have continued to follow through with your apartment search until you signed a lease.

- You could have borrowed/rented a backup computer to have on hand during your presentation. You also could have made backup files in case you had a problem with the computer or files. Or you might have you prepared paper handouts as a worst-case scenario substitute for your PowerPoint presentation.

CELEBRATE MAJOR AND MINOR ACHIEVEMENTS

Working out and following through with your plan can be stressful. Take time out to celebrate each victory.

- When someone pulls off his or her part of the plan, everybody should join in the celebration and success.

- Mark milestones with a celebration. Make sure you get together regularly for progress reports. When you reach your first week where everyone is right on schedule, pat yourselves on the back. Encourage each other and keep the end in plain sight.

- When you get any positive feedback on your plan, celebrate. The celebration might take the form of a presentation, illustrating the amazing effect of your master plan in action.

- Finally, when you've made it to the end and the problem is solved, don't forget to celebrate. Too often, that's when the team adjourns. Then the moment of shared

WHEN TO CELEBRATE

- At the one-week point

- At the one-month point

- With every individual success

- As you receive positive feedback to your plan

- When you reach an objective

- When you overcome an obstacle

- When you arrive at the end of the project

- Before you move on to the next project or assignment

Don't forget to celebrate with your coworkers when you solve a problem or complete a project. (ColorBlind Images, Corbis)

triumph is over, and the team has missed an opportunity to deepen team unity.

When students at a West Coast school spearheaded a local United Way drive, they took advantage of every opportunity to celebrate victories. All over the city, students set out thermometer signs, clearly marked with eight lines, each indicating a dollar amount. As contributions came in, students painted the thermometer in red to show how much money had been raised and how far they hoped to go. And whenever a school or business reached a new level, students celebrated. They showed up personally and congratulated participants.

Don't miss the chance to celebrate success.

LEARN FROM YOUR MISTAKES

Finally, the best way to grow as a problem solver is to learn from mistakes. You can learn from your own mistakes, from those of others, or from the mistakes of your company as a whole. Keep a notebook or a file of what you learn. Your experiences can do more

IT PAYS TO WORK TOGETHER

Groups of three to five people are much better at solving complex problems than even the most qualified and intelligent person working alone, according to a study published in the *Journal of Personality and Social Psychology,* a publication of the American Psychological Association.

"We found that groups of size three, four, and five outperformed the best individuals and attribute this performance to the ability of people to work together to generate and adopt correct responses, reject erroneous responses, and effectively process information," said lead study author Dr. Patrick Laughlin, of the University of Illinois at Urbana-Champaign, in a press release about the study.

for you than a whole book on problem solving (but only if you learn from your mistakes).

There are three classes of people in the world. The first learn from their own experience—these are wise; the second learn from the experience of others—these are happy; the third neither learn from their own experiences nor the experiences of others—these are fools.

—Philip Chesterfield, English
statesman and author

✍ EXERCISE

- Name three mistakes you've made in the past three years, and explain what you've learned from each mistake.

- What kinds of contingency plans do sports teams need? Wedding planners? Police during a public demonstration? Tour guides?

- Make a New Year's resolution. Imagine everything that might go wrong. What might you do to reduce the risk of not meeting your goal?

✔ TRUE OR FALSE: ANSWERS

Are You Ready to Follow Through?

1. When creating a plan to solve a problem, it's important to develop a contingency plan in case your original plan hits a roadblock.

True. Nothing ever goes as planned, so you should always have a backup plan ready in case you need it. It's not that difficult to devise a plan to fix a problem, but the mark of a good worker/team is the ability to be prepared for any contingency so that a project can proceed without delay.

2. Successful teams troubleshoot problems ahead of time.

True. It's a good idea to conduct a dry-run of your solution to a problem in order to ensure that you don't waste time, money, and staff once the plan is actually implemented.

3. There is no need to celebrate the accomplishment of goals. Just meeting them is enough of a reward.

False. Meeting objectives and goals deserves celebration at every level (whether a quick round of high-fives for meeting a project objective or a celebratory lunch for completing a major project goal). Taking the time to celebrate keeps morale up and workers focused on the big picture—especially on projects that last a long time.

IN SUMMARY . . .

- Once you develop your plan of action, and before your team begins the project, ask yourself what could go wrong with the plan. Try to anticipate every possible problem and develop a contingency plan.

- If at all possible, try out your plan before you commit all your resources. This will allow you to modify the plan's weak aspects before you get into the project.

- Even the best-laid plans will encounter roadblocks, speed bumps, and other challenges. Be flexible when you encounter problems and be willing to change your thinking to meet goals.

- Be persistent as you work toward project objectives. Don't accept no for an answer. Do everything you can to make the project a success.

- Learn from your mistakes, from the mistakes of others, and from the mistakes of your company as a whole. Keep a notebook of what went wrong and right during the project. Use these notes to help you learn from your mistakes.

• Take the time to celebrate project milestones, as well as the completion of the project. Celebrating milestones will build your team's confidence and allow you to stay focused on the big picture.

10

DECISION MAKING

Do you hate decisions? Do you buy only one brand of cereal because you can't stand making decisions early in the morning? Now that you have a method for solving problems, you also have a decision-making method. With a few minor adjustments, you can use the same steps to arrive at almost any decision.

In life, never spend more than 10 percent of your time on the problem, and spend at least 90 percent of your time on the solution.

—Fundamental rule of business

Let's see how the same five-step approach to problem solving works for making personal decisions. Suppose you have enough money saved to buy your first car. What are you going to choose?

✔ TRUE OR FALSE?

Can You Make a Decision?

1. There are three basic steps to decision making:
(1) Identify and define the decision to be made;
(2) Generate choices; and (3) Make the decision.

2. A rush to judgment is a major foe of decision making.

3. Making a list of pros and cons is one good way to help make a decision.

Test yourself as you read through this chapter. The answers appear on pages 164–165.

STEP 1—IDENTIFY AND DEFINE THE DECISION TO BE MADE

You stand on the threshold of your first car purchase. But to identify this necessary decision, you may have had to do a lot of thinking. Your questioning may have started with, "Should I take the bus or call my buddy?" "Should I walk or go back to bed?"

But you've sorted through the pile of questions and are determined to buy a car—some car, any car. Obviously, the decision is which car you should buy.

Or is it?

A good problem solver makes unpopular decisions when necessary, but considers the impact of decisions, remaining sensitive to other departments and individuals.

—**Human resources professional**

BOOKS ON DECISION MAKING

Adair, John. *Decision Making & Problem Solving Strategies.* 2d ed. London, U.K.: Kogan Page, 2007.

Decision Making: 5 Steps to Better Results. Boston, Mass.: Harvard Business School Press, 2006.

Gunther, Robert E., Stephen J. Hoch, and Howard C. Kunreuther. *Wharton on Making Decisions.* Hoboken, N.J.: Wiley, 2004.

Hammond, John S., Ralph L. Keeney, and Howard Raiffa. *Smart Choices: A Practical Guide to Making Better Decisions.* New York: Broadway Books, 2002.

Henderson, David R., Charles L. Hooper, and Mark Lawler. *Making Great Decisions in Business and Life.* Chicago Park, Calif.: Chicago Park Press, 2007.

SURF THE WEB: DECISION MAKING

Decision Making
http://www.decisionmaking.org

Mind Tools: Decision Making Techniques
http://www.mindtools.com/pages/main/newMN_
   TED.htm

STEP 2—WEIGH GOALS AND OBJECTIVES

As a business needs to relate its short-range goals to its long-term goals, or mission statement, you need to base your decision on your long-range goals, too. Check your short-term decisions against your long-term goals.

Your long-term goal may be to go to college. If you need this car money for your first year's tuition, you have another decision to make.

FIVE FOES OF DECISION MAKING

- Fear of failure
- Rush to judgment
- Laziness
- Short-sighted disregard for long-range goals
- Self-deception

But let's say you're not threatening your college career with the purchase. So you define the decision to be made: Which car shall I buy?

STEP 3—GENERATE CHOICES

Now you do your homework—your car buyer's homework, that is. You go through car showrooms, school parking lots, want ads, and websites that advertise cars. You list every possible car for sale in the United States and beyond.

The sky's the limit in your dream list. Leave that Porsche and Ferrari right where they are, at the top of the list. Keep going. Ask Uncle Chuck if he wants to sell his old Dodge. Are they still selling station wagons?

Remember, this is the brainstorming phase. No censuring allowed.

STEP 4—EVALUATE YOUR CHOICES

Now it's time to get real. Evaluate your choices according to your needs and ability. (You can still get the color you want.) The more information you have, the better. Try consulting *Consumer Reports,* the Internet, car owners, or a good mechanic.

☛ FACT

Intelligence is derived from two words—*inter* (meaning "between") and *legere* (meaning "to choose"). An intelligent person is one who learns to choose between or among options.

Making a list of pros and cons, or good and bad points, about your top choices may help you reach a decision. Imagine you've narrowed your list down to two possibilities: (1) buying your dad's Chevy or (2) buying a used Honda. Try making a chart like the one for "Dad's Chevy" on the next page.

Now make a similar list for the Honda. Then try to take an objective look at the strengths and weaknesses of each car.

Again and again, the impossible decision is solved when we see that the problem is only a tough decision waiting to be made.

—**Dr. Robert Schuller, U.S. minister**

DAD'S CHEVY

PROS	CONS
The price is right	Drive my dad's car?
New tires	Gas guzzler
No interest	Unexciting model
Known condition	Five years old

TIPS ON DECISION MAKING

• Clearly define the decision to be made.

• Evaluate your decisions by your long-term goals.

• Generate many possible decisions.

• Evaluate each possible answer.

• Make a list of pros and cons.

• Know that you may change your mind.

• Learn from your mistakes.

STEP 5—MAKE THE DECISION

The time will come when you must decide. Let's hope the decision-making process has clarified your choices and shown you what to do. Some of us still drag our feet and put off deciding as long as possible. Others tend to rush into everything. It will help you to know which way you lean.

Some people make decisions too quickly. If you're one of them, make yourself slow down. Don't come to snap decisions. Try to stay flexible for as long as you can. You'll waste more time trying to undo a wrong decision.

Delaying a decision is not the same as indecision, however. Some people are too slow to decide. If that's you, realize that many decisions can be changed quite easily. You have to move on something. It's easier to change the direction of a moving vehicle than one stuck in the mud. Even if you make a mistake, it's probably not the end of the world.

NO PROBLEM

Review the steps to problem solving:

- Step 1—Identify and define the problem.

- Step 2—Define goals and objectives.

- Step 3—Generate solutions.

- Step 4—Make a plan of action.

- Step 5—Follow through.

Don't forget that problems can turn into opportunities if you use both kinds of thinking—scientific and creative. Imagine the first guy who spilled bleach on his blue jeans and called it "stonewashed." Or how about the fellow who ran from his bathtub, screaming, "Eureka!" when he figured out the dis-

Don't forget that problems can turn into opportunities if you use both kinds of thinking— scientific and creative.

✐ EXERCISE

What's the biggest decision you're facing now? Run it through the five-step problem-solving process.

placement of water theory. Or consider Dr. Fleming, who returned to his lab and found a mold growing on a specimen slide. That problem turned into the discovery of penicillin.

Will you be one of those people who can say, "No problem" to difficulties? The decision is yours.

Men must be decided on what they will not do, and they are able to act with vigor in what they ought to do.

—Mencius, Confucian philosopher

TRUE OR FALSE: ANSWERS

Can You Make a Decision?

1. There are three basic steps to decision making: (1) Identify and define the decision to be made; (2) Generate choices; and (3) Make the decision.

False. There actually are five basic steps: (1) Identify and define the decision to be made; (2) Weigh goals and objectives; (3) Generate choices; (4) Evaluate your choices; and (5) Make the decision. If you skip "weigh goals and objectives," you won't have all the information necessary to make a good decision. If you forget to "evaluate your choices," you may be rushing through the decision-making process and end up making a poor decision.

2. A rush to judgment is a major foe of decision making.

True. Too often, people hurry through the decision-making process without determining why they need to make a decision, gathering enough information to make an educated decision, coming up with enough possible decision options, and determining what the results will be of each decision option.

3. Making a list of pros and cons is one good way to help make a decision.

True. This time-tested approach may be considered cliché, but it serves as a very effective way to help you determine why you should or should not make a decision.

IN SUMMARY . . .

- You can apply the five basic steps of problem solving to decision making, too. The five steps are:

    1. Identify and define the decision to be made.

    2. Weigh goals and objectives.

    3. Generate choices.

    4. Evaluate your choices.

    5. Make the decision.

- Creating a pro/con list is a great way to determine the strengths and weaknesses of a potential decision.

- The five foes of decision making are:

  1. fear of failure

  2. rushing to judgment

  3. laziness

  4. short-sighted disregard for long-range goals

  5. self-deception

- To make a decision, you need to be confident, deliberate, energetic, cognizant of long-term benefits, and honest with yourself.

- Delaying a decision is not the same as indecision.

- Problems can turn into opportunities if you use both scientific and creative thinking.

WEB SITES

Brainstorming

Brainstorming
  http://www.unc.edu/depts/wcweb/handouts/
  brainstorming.html

Brainstorming.co.uk
  http://www.brainstorming.co.uk/contents.html

Empowersu.com
  http://www.empowersu.com/articles/motivation-
  al/brainstorming-review.html

Mind Tools: Brainstorming
  http://www.mindtools.com/brainstm.html

Creativity

Creativity at Work
  http://www.creativityatwork.com

Creativity Foundation
  http://creativity-found.org/index.html

Creativity Portal
http://www.creativity-portal.com/bc

How to Unleash Your Creativity
http://www.sciam.com/article.cfm?id=how-to-unleash-your-creativity

Mind Tools: Creativity Tools
http://www.mindtools.com/pages/main/newMN_CT.htm

10 Steps for Boosting Creativity
http://www.jpb.com/creative/creative.php

10 Steps to a More Creative Office
http://www.jpb.com/creative/office_creativity.php

Decision Making

Decision Making
http://www.decisionmaking.org

Mind Tools: Decision Making Techniques
http://www.mindtools.com/pages/main/newMN_TED.htm

General

O*NET Online
http://online.onetcenter.org

Happiness/Positive Thinking

How to be Happy: Step-by-Step Guide to Being Happy
http://stress.about.com/od/lowstresslifestyle/ss/happy.htm

MayoClinic.com: Positive Thinking
http://www.mayoclinic.com/health/positive-thinking/SR00009

Mental Health, Self Help & Psychology Information and Resources
http://www.mental-health-matters.com

Mind Tools: Thought Awareness, Rational Thinking, and Positive Thinking
http://www.mindtools.com/redpstv.html

Positive Path Network
http://www.positivepath.net

SelfhelpMagazine
http://www.selfhelpmagazine.com/index.php

WebMD: Five Things Happy People Do
http://www.webmd.com/balance/features/five-things-happy-people-do

Logical Fallacies

The Autonomist: Logical Fallacies, Formal and Informal
http://theautonomist.com/aaphp/permanent/fallacies.php

Fallacy Files
http://www.fallacyfiles.org

LogicalFallacies.info
http://www.logicalfallacies.info

The Nizkor Project
http://www.nizkor.org/features/fallacies

Meetings

EffectiveMeetings.com
    http://www.effectivemeetings.com

Office Technology

Expert Village: Learn Basic Computer Skills
    http://www.expertvillage.com/video-series/528_
    computer-filing-system-windows.htm

How Stuff Works: How Fax Machines Work
    http://communication.howstuffworks.com/fax-
    machine4.htm

How Stuff Works: How Virtual Offices Work
    http://communication.howstuffworks.com/
    virtual-office.htm

How to Use a Scanner
    http://www.aarp.org/learntech/computers/
    howto/Articles/a2002-07-16-scan.html

Right Brain/Left Brain Thinking

Funderstanding: Right Brain vs. Left Brain
    http://www.funderstanding.com/right_left_
    brain.cfm

The Human Brain: The Left and Right Brains
    http://www.wright.edu/academics/honors/insti-
    tute/brain/leftright.html

Left or Right Brain
    http://www.angelfire.com/wi/2brains

Mathpower.com: Learning Styles, Culture &
Hemispheric Dominance
http://www.mathpower.com/brain.htm

Right Brain vs. Left Brain Creativity Test
http://www.wherecreativitygoestoschool.com/
vancouver/left_right/rb_test.htm

GLOSSARY

brainstorming the practice of quickly generating multiple ideas

clustering a brainstorming technique to help spill out flashes of inspiration in unplanned relationships; thoughts come out as clusters

contingency something that depends on unforeseen or accidental occurrences

convergent thinking logical, critical, analytical, straight-line, or predictable thinking; same as "scientific thinking"

creative thinking inspirational, divergent, insightful, exploratory, or unpredictable thinking; creative thinking rockets you through new, provocative channels to shed light on new answers to old problems

divergent thinking same as "creative thinking"

ex post facto faulty reasoning based on an assumed cause and effect

flowchart a chart that shows steps in a sequence of operations

freewriting a brainstorming technique that involves writing whatever comes to mind for a short duration of time

goal an end one strives to attain

hasty generalization the logical fallacy of assuming a connection between possibly unrelated events

hypothesis an opinion or theory to be tested

listing a brainstorming method that involves writing down ideas as fast as you can

logical fallacy errors in thinking

long-range goals goals that involve more detailed and complex planning and, consequently, take more time to reach

many-sided problems problems that combine difficulties involving people, organizations, and equipment

mechanical problems problems caused by computer software and hardware, telephone voice mail, machinery, and office equipment; also called technical problems

objectives usually small, specific steps that lead to a larger goal

organizational problems problems in the workplace that are out of an individual's control and that do not allow him or her to complete tasks; these might include the inability to get resources to complete a task, an unclear chain of command, economic or marketplace changes, and overlapping responses

people problems problems that involve yourself, one other person, or a group of people

poisoning the well hampering the credibility of people before they have an opportunity to present their cases

problem a situation, object, individual, or group that makes it hard to achieve an objective or goal

problem-solving skills techniques that help clarify thinking and get to the root of problems, thus enabling an effective solution

scientific thinking logical, critical, analytical, convergent, straight-line, and predictable thinking; it follows certain rules of logic from Point A through Point B to Point C

short-range goals goals that can be achieved in a short time

six Ws who, what, when, where, why, and what if; a method of analysis used to identify a problem

starbursting a brainstorming technique that focuses on generating questions to better understand a proposed product, service, or idea

SWOT test a test used to determine the true problem in a situation; **SWOT**=analyzing a situation for **s**trengths, **w**eaknesses, **o**pportunities, and seasonal **t**hreats

troubleshooting investigating, finding, and wiping out the source of trouble

visualization the practice of creating a mental picture

word association a brainstorming technique that involves responding immediately to a spoken or written word with another word; the word may or may not have a correlation to the first word; used to generate offbeat associations that may lead to a creative solution for a problem

BIBLIOGRAPHY

Adair, John. *Decision Making & Problem Solving Strategies*. 2d ed. London, U.K.: Kogan Page, 2007.

Bachel, Beverly K. *What Do You Really Want? How to Set a Goal and Go for It! A Guide for Teens*. Minneapolis, Minn.: Free Spirit Publishing, 2001.

Browne, M. Neil, and Stuart M. Keeley. *Asking the Right Questions: A Guide to Critical Thinking*. 8th ed. Upper Saddle River, N.J.: Prentice Hall, 2006.

Clegg, Brian, and Paul Birch. *Instant Creativity: Simple Techniques to Ignite Innovation & Problem Solving*. London, U.K.: Kogan Page, 2007.

Cory, Timothy R., and Thomas Slater. *Brainstorming: Techniques for New Ideas*. Bloomington, Ind.: iUniverse, 2003.

Decision Making: 5 Steps to Better Results. Boston: Harvard Business School Press, 2006.

Dobson, Michael S., and Susan B. Wilson. *Goal Setting: How to Create an Action Plan and Achieve Your Goals*. 2d ed. New York: AMACOM Books, 2008.

Fogler, H. Scott, and Steven E. LeBlanc. *Strategies for Creative Problem Solving.* 2d ed. Upper Saddle River, N.J.: Prentice Hall, 2007.

Foster, Jack, and Larry Corby. *How to Get Ideas.* 2d ed. San Francisco: Berrett-Koehler Publishers, 2007.

Gula, Robert J. Nonsense: *A Handbook of Logical Fallacies.* Mount Jackson, Va.: Axios Press, 2002.

Gunther, Robert E., Stephen J. Hoch, and Howard C. Kunreuther. *Wharton on Making Decisions.* Hoboken, N.J.: Wiley, 2004.

Hammond, John S., Ralph L. Keeney, and Howard Raiffa. *Smart Choices: A Practical Guide to Making Better Decisions.* New York: Broadway Books, 2002.

Harrison, Sam. *IdeaSpotting: How to Find Your Next Great Idea.* Cincinnati, Ohio: How Books, 2006.

Henderson, David R., Charles L. Hooper, and Mark Lawler. *Making Great Decisions in Business and Life.* Chicago Park, Calif.: Chicago Park Press, 2007

Higgins, James M. *101 Creative Problem Solving Techniques: The Handbook of New Ideas for Business.* Rev. ed. Winter Park, Fla.: New Management Publishing Company, 2005.

Kahane, Adam. *Solving Tough Problems: An Open Way of Talking, Listening, and Creating New Realities.* 2d ed. San Francisco: Berrett-Koehler Publishers, 2007.

Kreeft, Peter. *Socratic Logic: A Logic Text Using Socratic Method, Platonic Questions, and Aristotelian*

Principles. 3d ed. Chicago: St. Augustine's Press, 2008.

Lyubomirsky, Sonja. *The How of Happiness: A Scientific Approach to Getting the Life You Want.* New York: Penguin Press, 2007.

McCoy Jr., Charles W. *Why Didn't I Think of That? Think the Unthinkable and Achieve Creative Greatness.* Upper Saddle River, N.J.: Prentice Hall, 2002.

Michalko, Michael. *Thinkpak: A Brainstorming Card Deck.* Rev. ed. Berkeley, Calif.: Ten Speed Press, 2006.

Monahan, Tom. *The Do It Yourself Lobotomy: Open Your Mind to Greater Creative Thinking.* Hoboken, N.J.: Wiley, 2002.

Priest, Graham. *Logic: A Very Short Introduction.* New York: Oxford University Press, 2001.

Rich, Jason. *Brain Storm: Tap into Your Creativity to Generate Awesome Ideas and Remarkable Results.* Franklin Lakes, N.J.: Career Press, 2003.

Ries, Estelle H. *How To Get Ideas.* Whitefish, Mont.: Kessinger Publishing, LLC, 2007.

Roam, Dan. *The Back of the Napkin: Solving Problems and Selling Ideas with Pictures.* New York: Penguin, 2008.

Rouillard, Larrie. *Crisp: Goals and Goal Setting: Achieving Measured Objectives.* 3d ed. Florence, Ky.: Crisp Learning, 2002.

Russell, Ken, and Philip Carter. *Workout for a Balanced Brain.* New York: Readers Digest, 2001.

Souter, Nick. *Creative Business Solutions: Breakthrough Thinking: Brainstorming for Inspiration and Ideas.* New York: Sterling Publishing, 2007.

Tao, Terence. *Solving Mathematical Problems: A Personal Perspective.* New York: Oxford University Press, 2006.

Tracy, Brian. *Goals! How to Get Everything You Want—Faster Than You Ever Thought Possible.* San Francisco: Berrett-Koehler Publishers, 2004.

Treffinger, Donald J., Scott G. Isaksen, and K. Brian Stead-Dorval. *Creative Problem Solving: An Introduction.* 4th ed. Waco, Tex.: Prufrock Press, 2006.

Whyte, Jamie. *Crimes Against Logic: Exposing the Bogus Arguments of Politicians, Priests, Journalists, and Other Serial Offenders.* New York: McGraw-Hill, 2004.

Zaccaro, Edward. *Becoming a Problem Solving Genius: A Handbook of Math Strategies.* Bellevue, Iowa: Hickory Grove Press, 2006.

Zeitz, Paul. *The Art and Craft of Problem Solving.* Hoboken, N.J.: Wiley, 2006.

INDEX